High-Leverage Practices in Special Education

January 2017
The HLP Writing Team

James McLeskey (Chair)
University of Florida

Mary-Dean Barringer
Council of Chief State School Officers

Bonnie Billingsley
Virginia Polytechnic Institute and State University

Mary Brownell
University of Florida

Dia Jackson
American Institutes for Research

Michael Kennedy
University of Virginia

Tim Lewis
University of Missouri

Larry Maheady
SUNY Buffalo State

Jackie Rodriguez
William & Mary

Mary Catherine Scheeler
The Pennsylvania State University

Judy Winn
University of Wisconsin-Milwaukee

Deborah Ziegler
Council for Exceptional Children

Council for
Exceptional
Children

CEEDAR
CENTER

Council for Exceptional Children
2900 Crystal Drive, Suite 100
Arlington, VA 22202-3557
www.cec.sped.org

Permission is granted to reproduce and adapt any portion of this publication with acknowledgment.
Reference:

McLeskey, J., Barringer, M-D., Billingsley, B., Brownell, M., Jackson, D., Kennedy, M., Lewis, T., Maheady, L., Rodriguez, J., Scheeler, M. C., Winn, J., & Ziegler, D. (2017, January). *High-leverage practices in special education.* Arlington, VA: Council for Exceptional Children & CEEDAR Center.

This document was supported from funds provided by the CEEDAR Center (Collaboration for Effective Educator, Development, Accountability and Reform) cooperative grant supported by the Office of Special Education Programs (OSEP) of the U.S. Department of Education (H325A120003). Drs. Bonnie Jones and David Guardino served as the project officers. The views expressed herein do not necessarily represent the positions or policies of the U.S. Department of Education. No official endorsement by the U.S. Department of Education of any product, commodity, or enterprise mentioned in this document is intended or should be inferred.

Library of Congress Cataloging-in-Publication data

Council for Exceptional Children and CEEDAR Center.
High-leverage practices in special education: Foundations for student success.
p. cm.
Includes biographical references.

ISBN 978-0-86586-526-6 (soft cover)
ISBN 978-0-86586-527-3 (eBook)

Stock No. P6255

Cover and layout by Tom Karabatakis, TomPromo Marketing
Printed in the United States of America by Bradford & Bigelow

First edition

10 9 8 7 6 5 4 3 2 1

Contents

Preface

Special education teachers, as a significant segment of the teaching profession, came into their own with the passage of Public Law 94-142, the Education for All Handicapped Children Act, in 1975. Since then, although the number of special education teachers has grown substantially it has not kept pace with the demand for their services and expertise. The roles and practice of special education teachers have continuously evolved as the complexity of struggling learners unfolded, along with the quest for how best to serve and improve outcomes for this diverse group of students.

As this complexity was addressed, those preparing special education teachers found themselves responding to conflicting external forces. New content was added to preparation programs to meet requirements of professional accreditation groups, changing state licensure requirements, and federal regulations related to teacher preparation. These programs also needed to respond to the long-term shortage of special education teachers, with intensive and rapid preparation of "highly qualified" teachers—although there was no clear guidance as to the most effective practices to target. Without clarity regarding the practices and expertise that define an *effective special educator*, this role began to be viewed by

potential teachers as less desirable than other teaching assignments despite the clear need and job assurance.

Meanwhile, research continued to establish evidence regarding practices that could make a positive difference with students who were struggling to find success in school because of learning and behavioral complexities. What was needed was guidance as to the most important of these practices that special educators needed to learn to use in classrooms—clear signals among the noise of demands placed on teacher education programs.

Development of the High-Leverage Practices in Special Education

In fall 2014, the Board of Directors of the Council for Exceptional Children (CEC) approved a proposal from the CEC Professional Standards and Practice Committee (PSPC) to develop a set of high-leverage practices (HLPs) for special education teachers. The PSPC, the Teacher Education Division (TED) of CEC, and the CEEDAR Center at the University of Florida endorsed this project. The CEEDAR Center, which is funded by the U.S. Department of Education's Office of Special Education Programs, provided a sub-award to CEC to support this work. The HLP Writing Team's 12 members included representatives from CEC's PSPC, TED, the CEEDAR Center, the Council of Chief State School Officers, and CEC staff. In addition, seven CEC members were selected from over 50 nominations that were received from the PSPC, TED, and the CEEDAR Center. This team of practitioners, scholars, researchers, teacher preparation faculty, and advocates knew that to achieve the project's intended purposes, they needed to ensure that the results of their work established the need to improve teacher preparation programs, provided a rationale both for developing practice-based teacher preparation programs and for the HLPs themselves, and explained how the HLPs could be used to support student learning.

The fundamental purpose of CEC's HLP project was to identify improved methods for supporting special education

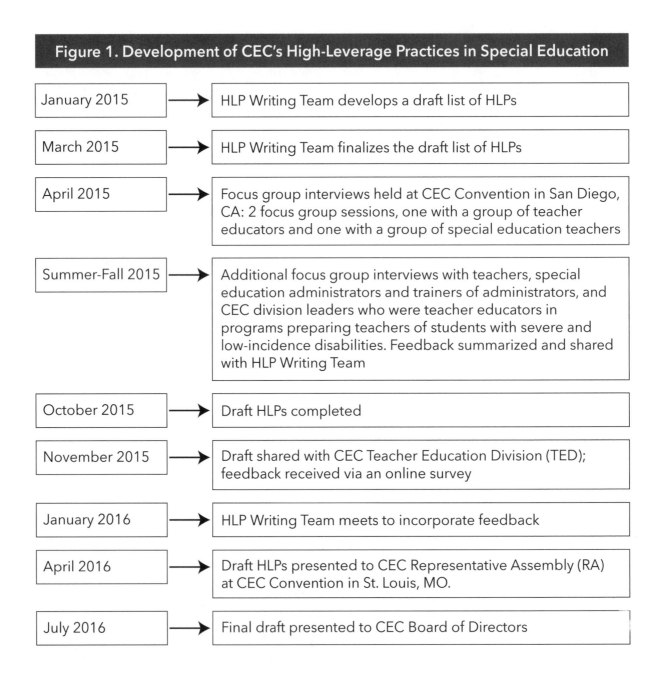

Figure 1. Development of CEC's High-Leverage Practices in Special Education

January 2015	→	HLP Writing Team develops a draft list of HLPs
March 2015	→	HLP Writing Team finalizes the draft list of HLPs
April 2015	→	Focus group interviews held at CEC Convention in San Diego, CA: 2 focus group sessions, one with a group of teacher educators and one with a group of special education teachers
Summer-Fall 2015	→	Additional focus group interviews with teachers, special education administrators and trainers of administrators, and CEC division leaders who were teacher educators in programs preparing teachers of students with severe and low-incidence disabilities. Feedback summarized and shared with HLP Writing Team
October 2015	→	Draft HLPs completed
November 2015	→	Draft shared with CEC Teacher Education Division (TED); feedback received via an online survey
January 2016	→	HLP Writing Team meets to incorporate feedback
April 2016	→	Draft HLPs presented to CEC Representative Assembly (RA) at CEC Convention in St. Louis, MO.
July 2016	→	Final draft presented to CEC Board of Directors

teacher candidates as they learn to use effective practices in their classrooms. Although effective teaching practices had previously been identified, these mainly comprised undifferentiated, overall lists with brief descriptions of each practice (e.g., teachingworks.org).

Figure 1 describes the development of the HLPs. The HLP Writing Team spent considerable time determining the group of special educators to whom the HLPs would apply. It was the perspective of the HLP Writing Team that a high-quality set of HLPs could be developed that directly applied to the classroom practices of teachers in K–12 settings, although a separate set of HLPs could be developed to more specifically address the particular practices used by teachers of students with gifts and talents. CEC's Division for Early Childhood has developed *DEC Recommended Practices* (2015), which provides guidance to practitioners and families about the most effective ways to improve the learning outcomes and development of young children, birth through age 5, who have or are at risk for developmental delays or disabilities.

The HLPs are organized around four aspects of practice—collaboration, assessment, social/emotional/behavioral practices, and instruction—because special education teachers enact practices in these areas in integrated and reciprocal ways. For example, special education teachers use assessment to design instruction and then evaluate it. The HLPs for instruction can be used to teach both academic content and emotional, behavioral, and social skills; special education teachers bring their knowledge of HLPs in these areas to collaboration with other professionals and parents.

The integrated and recursive use of HLPs in these four areas results in some overlap at times; for example, to learn to use the collaboration HLPs in practice requires teachers to have a deep know

ledge of practices related to each of the other three areas. Similarly, using assessment data to make instructional decisions is a critical component of both effective instruction and effective assessment. Providing effective feedback appears in both the social/emotional/behavioral practices HLPs and the instruction HLPs; two research syntheses were developed as the basis for this item. Organizing the HLPs in this way was intended to make them more comprehensible and easier to use in planning core components of a practice-based teacher preparation program.

It should be noted that CEC's HLPs, and their incorporation of culturally responsive approaches, might also be considered effective practice for general education teachers. However, the manner in which these practices are enacted by special educators differs from how they are enacted by general education teachers. For example, general education teachers are expected to use different types of assessment information (e.g., performance on state assessments, work samples, informal conversations with students, observations) to improve their understanding of students in their classrooms. The extent to which special education teachers are expected to collect assessment information and develop a learner profile is different. Special education teachers are expected to:

- collect detailed information about students,
- develop detailed processes for tracking the progress students are making,
- ensure that students' families' and general education teachers' understandings are incorporated in the collection of information and its use in designing instruction, and
- be thorough in the use of assessment data to design and evaluate instruction tailored carefully to students' needs.

Effective instruction by special education teachers requires a deep and comprehensive understanding of students with disabilities that allows them to develop highly responsive, explicit, systematic instructional and behavioral interventions that support the success of these students and responds to their diverse and complex needs.

High-Leverage Practices in Special Education only scratches the surface in addressing the many issues that will arise in enacting this new vision of teacher preparation. Indeed, it is hoped that the HLPs are perceived as a working and evolving set of practices that can be used as teacher educators collectively develop an understanding of core practices, determine how such practices may be best used, and identify how they can be improved.

The HLPs are intended to provide those who work in school districts in beginning teacher induction and residency programs, or who provide professional development for teachers of students with disabilities, with a clear vision of effective teaching for these students. Administrators and principals who provide professional development for special education teachers—and, arguably, for *all* teachers who teach students with disabilities—can use these HLPs to select experiences where evidence shows that skillfulness in using practices makes a difference for student success. The HLPs provide families with clarity about effective practices that can improve educational outcomes for their children. Policy makers may use this guidance to focus their efforts on the most important practices as they consider teacher licensure requirements, micro-credentialing opportunities, or guidelines for approving teacher preparation programs. And, ultimately—from a prospective teacher's perspective—this is a playbook that describes the foundational practices needed for an effective and suc-

cessful career creating success stories for our nation's students with the most complex learning and behavioral needs.

Acknowledgments

The members of the HLP Writing Team express their appreciation to Lorraine Sobson from CEC for the fine work she did in pulling together the disparate components of this document in a logical and coherent way. In addition, thanks to the Office of Special Education Programs for their support of this project and devotion to improving instructional practice in special education. Finally, the HLP Writing Team expresses appreciation to the following individuals, who assisted the Team in developing the high-leverage practices, including participating in feedback sessions, writing, and reviewing content:

Sheila Alber-Morgan
Ohio State University

Tammy Barron
West Carolina University

Elizabeth Bettini
Boston University

Jean Crockett
University of Florida

Rebecca Zumeta Edmunds
American Institutes of Research

Marilyn Friend
University of North Carolina-Greensboro

Kharon Grimmet
Purdue University

Charles Hughes
The Pennsylvania State University

Meg Kamman
University of Florida

Holly Lane
University of Florida

David Lee
The Pennsylvania State University

Erica Lembke
University of Missouri

Troy Mariage
Michigan State University

Kristen McMaster
University of Minnesota

Kathleen Paliokas
Interstate Teacher Assessment and Support Consortium (InTASC)

Yujeong Park
University of Tennessee

Donna Sacco
George Mason University

Karrie A. Shogren
University of Kansas

George Sugai
University of Connecticut

Jocelyn Washburn
Virginia Polytechnic Institute and State University

Joe Wehby
Vanderbilt University

Pamela Williamson
University of North Carolina-Greensboro

References

CEC Division for Early Childhood. (2015). *DEC recommended practices: Enhancing services for young children with disabilities and their families.* Arlington, VA: Author.

Introduction

Skillful teaching requires appropriately using and integrating specific moves and activities in particular cases and contexts, based on knowledge and understanding of one's pupils and on the application of professional judgment.

(Ball & Forzani, 2009, p. 497)

Concerns about achievement levels of students who struggle in school, including those with disabilities, have led to major changes in U.S. education policy. These changes have included increased expectations and accountability for student achievement and calls for improving the practice of teachers (e.g., the Every Student Succeeds Act of 2015 and its predecessor, the No Child Left Behind Act of 2001; NCATE, 2010; U.S. Department of Education, 2010). Improving teacher practice has become a major focus of policy makers and teacher educators for several reasons, including research revealing that (a) improving the effectiveness of teachers is the most direct approach to improving outcomes for low-achieving students (Hanushek & Rivkin, 2010; Master, Loeb, & Wyckoff, 2014), and that (b) many effective practices that can substantially improve student achievement are not routinely used by teachers (Cook & Odom, 2013).

The need to improve teacher practice has led several prominent teacher educators (e.g., Ball & Forzani, 2011; Grossman, Hammerness, & McDonald, 2009; Leko, Brownell, Sindelar, & Kiely, 2015; McDonald, Kazemi, & Kavanaugh, 2013) to take the position that teacher education should focus more deliberately on instructional practice, and that teacher preparation programs should be developed that address this goal. In these programs, teacher education would be centered on a set of effective practices that all teachers need to learn (i.e., practices that are used frequently in classrooms and have been shown to improve student outcomes). Programs also would embed much of teacher preparation in clinical settings to systematically support teacher candidates in learning to use these HLPs (Grossman et al., 2009; NCATE, 2010). This emphasis on using practice-based teacher education to improve instructional practice has emerged in both general and special education (Leko et al., 2015; McDonald et al., 2013).

Effective Special Education Teachers

Learning to teach is complex and demanding work. Although all beginning teachers are challenged to teach in ways that are responsive to students' needs, special education teachers face the challenge of teaching students with some of the most complex learning and behavioral difficulties. These students have some combination of attention, memory, reasoning, communication, physical, and behavioral difficulties that can interfere with their ability to acquire the literacy, numeracy, independent living, and social skills needed to be successful in schools, postsecondary education, and work environments (Klingner et al., 2016). Moreover, students with disabilities have diverse needs that may include one or a combination of academic difficulties or emotional and behavioral challenges in schools. The severity of these challenges varies substantially. For example, whereas some students with disabilities have complex and pervasive physical and cognitive disabilities and may require extensive support throughout much of the school day, other students struggle with a specific content area, require much more focused support, and may have grade-level or advanced skills in other content areas. Further, a disproportionate number of students with disabilities are from high-poverty settings or from culturally and linguistically diverse backgrounds (Klingner et al., 2016).

Many students with disabilities have failed to make sufficient progress in the general education classroom. Although general education teachers must be responsive to the needs of students with disabilities, effective instruction by special education teachers requires a deeper and more comprehensive understanding of students that facilitates the development of highly responsive, explicit, systematic instructional and behavioral interventions that support the success of these students. To ensure quality outcomes for students with disabilities, special education teachers should provide instruction that is evidence-based and highly responsive to these students' complex and varied needs. Special education teachers must be flexible problem solvers who not only have expertise in using highly effective practices, but also are proficient in monitoring the effectiveness of these practices with individual students and making decisions regarding changes in practice as needed. This routine analysis of practice and its effect on important student outcomes is foundational for effective special education teachers. Further, given the disproportionate number of students with disabilities from culturally and linguistically diverse backgrounds, special education teachers must have expertise in delivering instruction and behavioral interventions in a culturally responsive manner (Aronson & Laughter, 2016).

Given the complexity of this work, preparing special education teachers who are ready to use effective practices as soon as they begin teaching is a daunting task. Beginning special education teachers require coherent and repeated opportunities to both apply their knowledge in realistic settings and receive feedback regarding their practice (Leko et al., 2015). Such deliberate practice in authentic contexts is essential to the development of effective performance and skilled decision making in

> *Special education teachers must be flexible problem solvers who not only have expertise in using highly effective practices, but also are proficient in monitoring the effectiveness of these practices with individual students and making decisions regarding changes in practice as needed.*

many professions (e.g., nursing, plumbing, the military), and teaching students with disabilities is no different. To engage in this type of practice-based teacher education, teacher educators need to identify a limited number of critical practices that all special educators can use in classrooms, and those practices should become the core curriculum of teacher preparation programs.

High-Leverage Practices and Practice-Based Teacher Education

Aspiring special education teachers need opportunities to learn those practices that are essential to promoting improved outcomes for students with disabilities if they are to be prepared to use these practices when they enter classrooms. Teacher candidates can only learn so much during their preparation programs, particularly if the goal is to develop fluency in employing complex practices that are responsive to the needs of students with disabilities. Given these limitations, they should learn to enact the most essential dimensions of effective practice, and they need focused learning opportunities where they can repeatedly practice these essential dimensions with close supervision and feedback to do this.

Ball and colleagues (Ball & Forzani, 2011; Grossman et al., 2009; McDonald et al., 2013) have referred to these essential dimensions of instruction as *high-leverage practices* (HLPs). In short, these are practices that can be used to leverage student learning across different content areas, grade levels, and student abilities and disabilities. For instance, HLPs might be used to teach evidence-based practices (e.g., using explicit instruction to teach and practice a

> *Professionals learn best when they have repeated opportunities to practice the essential components of effective performance, receive feedback on their performance, and receive support in analyzing and improving their performance.*

summarization strategy) at differing intensity levels and across tiers of instruction. HLPs also might be the fundamental skills needed to collaborate effectively with other educators and families.

The criteria that were used to select CEC's HLPs for K–12 special education teachers are included in Table 1 (cf. Ball, Sleep, Boerst, & Bass, 2009; Grossman et al., 2009; McDonald et al., 2013; Windschitl, Thompson, Braaten, & Stroupe, 2012). In short, these practices must represent the essence of effective practice in special education. Further, from the perspective of teacher preparation programs, these should be practices that novices can learn, and which can be taught to a reasonable level of proficiency during the course of a teacher preparation program.

The HLPs can become the foundation of a cohesive, practice-based teacher education curriculum that incorporates repeated, scaffolded, effective opportunities for special education teacher candidates to practice (Leko et al., 2015). Currently, many special education teacher education programs, like their general education counterparts, cover a broad range of topics rather than a focused set of practices that aspiring teachers are taught to use effectively (Goe, 2006; McLeskey & Brownell, 2015). Further, most of the learning in teacher education programs occurs in coursework, and is largely divorced from practice in Pre-K–12 schools. The primary practice opportunities teacher candidates currently have occur once they are in field placements in schools. Too often, teacher educators have insufficient influence over the quality of those opportunities, and the types of skills teacher candidates learn in them (Grossman & McDonald, 2008;

Table 1. Criteria for Identifying CEC's High-Leverage Practices	
Applicable and important to the everyday work of teachers	• Focus directly on instructional practice • Occur with high frequency in teaching • Research-based and known to foster important kinds of student engagement and learning • Broadly applicable and usable in any content area or approach to teaching • So important that skillfully executing them is fundamental to effective teaching

Applicable and important to teacher education	• Limited in number (about 20) for a teacher education program
	• Can be articulated and taught
	• Novices can begin to master
	• Can be practiced across university and field-based settings
	• Grain size (i.e., how detailed should the practice be) is small enough to be clearly visible in practice, but large enough to preserve the integrity and complexity of teaching
	• System (or group of HLP) considerations
	  ◦ embody a broader theory regarding the relationship between teaching and learning than would individual practices
	  ◦ support more comprehensive student learning goals (the whole is more than the sum of its parts)

McDonald et al., 2013; McLeskey & Brownell, 2015). Inadequate opportunities for teacher candidates to practice are problematic when considering research on professional learning in other fields. Studies of training in medicine, music, the military, and sports have shown that professionals learn best when they have repeated opportunities to practice the essential components of effective performance, receive feedback on their performance, and receive support in analyzing and improving their performance (Ericcson, 2014).

The HLPs provide an anchor for teacher educators and other preparation providers that enable them to design a focused curriculum that integrates coordinated, effective practice opportunities that are threaded throughout the program. These practices, and ways of increasing special education teachers' sophisticated use of them in different content areas (e.g., reading and mathematics) become the foundation for developing a cohesive approach to educating these teachers from initial preparation to induction and beyond. The use of focused, deliberate approaches to educating teachers over time is more aligned with effective practices in professional preparation that occur in other professions. Most important, this type of practice-based approach to teacher education produces beginning special education teachers who are prepared to engage in the types of complex instructional practice and professional collaborations that are required for educating students with disabilities effectively.

Identifying HLPs in special education has the potential to substantially improve teacher preparation and, ultimately, outcomes for students with disabilities and others who struggle to succeed in school. This new direction in teacher preparation (cf. Ball & Forzani, 2011; Grossman, Hammerness, & McDonald, 2009) reflects the core values that have provided the foundation of special education instruction for many years: That is, if someone needs to learn something, the special educator should identify what the person needs to learn, and provide systematic instruction until the learning is demonstrated. The establishment of HLPs in the field of special education has the potential to provide many benefits for teacher preparation in bridging research and practice and helping the field

> (a) articulate a common language for specifying practice, which would facilitate the field's ability to engage in collective activity; (b) identify and specify common pedagogies in teacher education; and (c) address the perennial and persistent divides among university courses and between university course work and clinical experiences. (McDonald, Kazemi, & Kavanaugh, 2013, p. 378)

Collective action among those who prepare teachers and provide continuing professional development is needed to enact this new vision of teacher preparation and professional development. There are obvious risks involved, primary among them the possibility that (as has occurred in the past with major initiatives to improve teacher preparation) there will be a "proliferation of approaches driven more by the trend than by

a deep understanding of how people learn to enact ambitious professional practice" (McDonald et al., 2013, p. 379). Given this history, those in the field must—albeit with caution—begin to enact this new vision of teacher preparation, which promises to build bridges between schools and teacher preparation programs and improve the preparation of teachers in ways that will substantially benefit students with disabilities and others who struggle in schools.

About This Publication

The primary purpose of *High-Leverage Practices in Special Education* is to provide those involved in special education teacher preparation and professional development with a set of HLPs that were identified through consensus among special educators. These HLPs may be used to design a cohesive set of practice based opportunities to support teacher candidates and practicing teachers in learning to put this know-how to use on behalf of the complex learners they teach.

In the following section, CEC's HLPs are provided across four intertwined components of special education teacher practice—collaboration, assessment, social/emotional/behavioral practices, and instruction. The 22 HLPs are intended to address the most critical practices that every K–12 special education teacher should master. The Research Syntheses that follow the HLPs delve more deeply into the rationale and evidence base for each. (As discussed in the Preface, two research syntheses were developed for the practice of providing effective feedback; this item appears in both the Social/Emotional/Behavioral Practices HLPs and the Instruction HLPs.) The appendices provide references for teacher educators, administrators, and teachers alike, with a glossary of terms and additional resources for each of the HLP components.

References

Aronson, B., & Laughter, J. (2016). The theory and practice of culturally relevant education: A synthesis of research across content areas. *Review of Educational Research, 86*, 163-205. doi:10.3102/0034654315582066

Ball, D., & Forzani, F. (2009). The work of teaching and the challenge of teacher education. *Journal of Teacher Education, 60*, 497-511. doi:10.1177/0022487109348479

Ball, D. & Forzani, F. (2011). Building a common core for learning to teach: And connecting professional learning to practice. *American Educator, 35*(2), 17-21, 38-39.

Ball, D. L., Sleep, L., Boerst, T., & Bass, H. (2009). Combining the development of practice and the practice of development in teacher education. *Elementary School Journal, 109*, 458-476. doi:10.1086/596996

Cook, B. & Odom, S. (2013). Evidence-based practices and implementation science in special education. *Exceptional Children, 79*, 135-144.

Ericcson, K. (2014). *The road to excellence: The acquisition of expert performance in the arts and sciences, sports and games.* New York, NY: Taylor & Francis.

Goe, L. (2006). *The teacher preparation-teacher practices-student outcomes relationship in special education: Missing links and next steps. A research synthesis.* Washington, DC: National Comprehensive Center for Teacher Quality. Retrieved from https://www.relcentral.org/resource-download/?id=1333&post_id=1332

Grossman, P., Hammerness, K., & McDonald, M. (2009). Redefining teaching: Re-imagining teacher education. *Teachers and teaching: Theory and Practice, 15*, 273-290. doi:10.1080/13540600902875340

Grossman, P., & McDonald, M. (2008). Back to the future: Directions for research in teaching and teacher education. *American Educational Research Journal, 45*, 184-205. doi:10.3102/0002831207312906

Hanushek, E. A., & Rivkin, S. G. (2010). Generalizations about using value-added measures of teacher quality. *American Economic Review: Papers and Proceedings, 100*, 267-271. doi:10.1257/aer.100.2.267

Klingner, J. K., Brownell, M. T., Mason, L. H., Sindelar, P. T., Benedict, A. E., Griffin, G. G., Lane, K., … Park, Y. (2016). Teaching students with special needs in the new millenium. In D. Gitomer & C. Bell (Eds.), *Handbook of research on teaching* (5th ed., pp. 639-717). Washington, DC: American Educational Research Association.

Leko, M., Brownell, M., Sindelar, P., & Kiely, M. (2015). Envisioning the future of special education personnel preparation in a standards-based era. *Exceptional Children, 82*, 25–43. doi:10.1177/0014402915598782

Master, B., Loeb, S., & Wyckoff, J. (2014). *Learning that lasts: Unpacking variation in teachers'effects on students' long-term knowledge* (Working Paper 104). New York, NY: Calder Urban Institute. New York: Calder Urban Institute. Retrieved from http://curry.virginia.edu/uploads/resourceLibrary/22_Master_Learning_that_Lasts.pdf

McDonald, M., Kazemi, E., & Kavanaugh, S. (2013). Core practices of teacher education: A call for a common language and collective activity. *Journal of Teacher Education, 64*, 378–386. doi:10.1177/0022487113493807

McLeskey, J., & Brownell, M. (2015). *High leverage practices and teacher preparation in special education*. Gainesville, FL: CEEDAR Center. Retrieved from http://ceedar.education.ufl.edu/wp-content/uploads/2016/05/High-Leverage-Practices-and-Teacher-Preparation-in-Special-Education.pdf

NCATE. (2010, November). *Transforming teacher education through clinical practice: A national strategy to prepare effective teachers. Report of the Blue Ribbon Panel on Clinical Preparation and Partnerships for Improved Student Learning*. Washington, DC: National Council for Accreditation of Teacher Education (NCATE). Retrieved from http://www.ncate.org/LinkClick.aspx?fileticket=zzeiB1OoqPk%3D&tabid=7

U.S. Department of Education. (2010). *A blueprint for reform. The reauthorization of the Elementary and Secondary Education Act*. Washington, DC: Author. https://www2.ed.gov/policy/elsec/leg/blueprint/blueprint.pdf

Windschitl, M., Thompson, J., Braaten, M., & Stroupe, D. (2012). Proposing a core set of instructional practices and tools for teachers of science. *Science Education, 96*, 878–903. 10.1002/sce.21027

High-Leverage Practices for K-12 Special Education Teachers

The high-leverage practices in special education (HLPs) are provided across four intertwined components of teacher practice: collaboration, assessment, social/emotional/behavioral practices, and instruction. The 22 HLPs are intended to address the most critical practices that every K-12 special education teacher should master. The Research Syntheses that follow this section delve more deeply into the rationale and evidence base for each. (As discussed in the Preface, two research syntheses were developed for the practice of providing effective feedback; this item appears in both the Social/Emotional/Behavioral Practices HLPs and the Instruction HLPs.) The appendix provides a glossary of terms and additional resources for each of the HLP components. Additional resources are available on CEC's HLP website.

Collaboration

Effective special education teachers collaborate with a wide range of professionals, families and caregivers to assure that educational programs and related services are effectively designed and implemented to meet the needs of each student with a disability. Collaboration allows for varied expertise and perspectives about a student to be shared among those responsible for the student's learning and well-being. This collective expertise provides collaborators with a more comprehensive understanding of each student's needs, which can be used to more effectively plan and implement instruction and services.

Teachers use respectful and effective communication skills as they collaborate with others, considering the background, socioeconomic status, culture, and language of the families and the professionals with whom they work. Collaborative activities should be focused on (a) designing each student's instructional program to meet clearly specified outcomes and (b) collecting data and monitoring progress toward these outcomes. Effective and purposeful collaboration should enlist support from district and school leaders, who can foster a collective commitment to collaboration, provide professional learning experiences to increase team members' collaborative skills, and create schedules that support different forms of ongoing collaboration (e.g., individualized education program [IEP] teams, co-teachers, teachers–families, teachers–paraprofessionals).

Assessment

Assessment plays a foundational role in special education. Students with disabilities are complex learners who have unique needs that exist alongside their strengths. Effective special education teachers have to fully understand those strengths and needs. Thus, these teachers are knowledgeable regarding assessment and are skilled in using and interpreting data. This includes formal, standardized assessments that are used in identifying students for special education services, developing students' IEPs, and informing ongoing services. Formal assessments such as statewide exams also provide data regarding whether students with disabilities are achieving state content standards and how their academic progress compares to students without disabilities. Teachers are also knowledgeable about and skillful in using informal assessments, such as those used to evaluate students' academic, behavioral, and functional strengths and needs. These assessments are used to develop students' IEPs, design and evaluate instruction, and monitor student progress. As reflective practitioners, special educators also continuously analyze the effect and effectiveness of their own instruction. Finally, these teachers are knowledgeable regarding how context, culture, language, and poverty might influence student performance; navigating conversations with families and other stakeholders; and choosing appropriate assessments given each student's profile. This is an especially important consideration, given the overrepresentation of culturally and linguistically diverse students and those from high poverty backgrounds in special education (see Linn & Hemmer, 2011; U.S. Department of Education, 2016; Zhang & Katisyannis, 2002).

Social/Emotional/Behavioral Practices

Effective special education teachers establish a consistent, organized, and respectful learning environment to support student success. To do this, they employ several practices that are critical in promoting student social and emotional well-being. First, effective teachers focus on increasing appropriate behavior by adopting an instructional approach that incorporates the explicit teaching of social skills and offers students multiple opportunities to practice appropriate social behaviors throughout the school day followed by positive specific feedback. Second, they implement evidence-based practices to prevent social, emotional, and behavioral challenges and provide early intervention at the first sign of risk. Third, effective teachers provide increasingly comprehensive supports through a team-based problem-solving strategy, to match the intensity of student challenges guided by behavioral assessment. Finally, they implement all behavioral supports—even those in response to significant problem behavior—in a caring, respectful, and culturally relevant manner. Effective teachers recognize that academic and behavioral support strategies are more effective when delivered within the context of positive and caring teacher–student relationships.

Instruction

Teaching students with disabilities is a strategic, flexible, and recursive process as effective special education teachers use content knowledge, pedagogical knowledge (including evidence-based practice), and data on student learning to design, deliver, and evaluate the effectiveness of instruction. This process begins with well-designed instruction. Effective special education teachers are well versed in general education curricula and other contextually relevant curricula, and use appropriate standards, learning progressions, and evidence-based practices in conjunction with specific IEP goals and benchmarks to prioritize long- and short-term learning goals and to plan instruction. This instruction, when delivered with fidelity, is designed to maximize academic learning time, actively engage learners in meaningful activities, and emphasize proactive and positive approaches across tiers of instructional intensity.

Effective special education teachers base their instruction and support of students with disabilities on the best available evidence, combined with their professional judgment and knowledge of individual student needs. Teachers value diverse perspectives and incorporate knowledge about students' backgrounds, culture, and language in their instructional decisions. Their decisions result in improved student outcomes across varied curriculum areas and in multiple educational settings. They use teacher-led, peer-assisted, student-regulated, and technology-assisted practices fluently, and know when and where to apply them. Analyzing instruction in this way allows teachers to improve student learning and their professional practice.

The High-Leverage Practices in Special Education

Collaboration

HLP1   **Collaborate with professionals to increase student success.**

Collaboration with general education teachers, paraprofessionals, and support staff is necessary to support students' learning toward measurable outcomes and to facilitate students' social and emotional well-being across all school environments and instructional settings (e.g., co-taught). Collaboration with individuals or teams requires the use of effective collaboration behaviors (e.g., sharing ideas, active listening, questioning, planning, problem solving, negotiating) to develop and adjust instructional or behavioral plans based on student data, and the coordination of expectations, responsibilities, and resources to maximize student learning.

Collaboration (cont'd)

HLP2	**Organize and facilitate effective meetings with professionals and families.**

Teachers lead and participate in a range of meetings (e.g., meetings with families, individualized education program [IEP] teams, individualized family services plan [IFSP] teams, instructional planning) with the purpose of identifying clear, measurable student outcomes and developing instructional and behavioral plans that support these outcomes. They develop a meeting agenda, allocate time to meet the goals of the agenda, and lead in ways that encourage consensus building through positive verbal and nonverbal communication, encouraging the sharing of multiple perspectives, demonstrating active listening, and soliciting feedback.

HLP3	**Collaborate with families to support student learning and secure needed services.**

Teachers collaborate with families about individual children's needs, goals, programs, and progress over time and ensure families are informed about their rights as well as about special education processes (e.g., IEPs, IFSPs). Teachers should respectfully and effectively communicate considering the background, socioeconomic status, language, culture, and priorities of the family. Teachers advocate for resources to help students meet instructional, behavioral, social, and transition goals. In building positive relationships with students, teachers encourage students to self-advocate, with the goal of fostering self-determination over time. Teachers also work with families to self-advocate and support their children's learning.

Assessment

HLP4	Use multiple sources of information to develop a comprehensive understanding of a student's strengths and needs.

To develop a deep understanding of a student's learning needs, special educators compile a comprehensive learner profile through the use of a variety of assessment measures and other sources (e.g., information from parents, general educators, other stakeholders) that are sensitive to language and culture, to (a) analyze and describe students' strengths and needs and (b) analyze the school-based learning environments to determine potential supports and barriers to students' academic progress. Teachers should collect, aggregate, and interpret data from multiple sources (e.g., informal and formal observations, work samples, curriculum-based measures, functional behavior assessment [FBA], school files, analysis of curriculum, information from families, other data sources). This information is used to create an individualized profile of the student's strengths and needs.

HLP5	Interpret and communicate assessment information with stakeholders to collaboratively design and implement educational programs.

Teachers interpret assessment information for stakeholders (i.e., other professionals, families, students) and involve them in the assessment, goal development, and goal implementation process. Special educators must understand each assessment's purpose, help key stakeholders understand how culture and language influence interpretation of data generated, and use data to collaboratively develop and implement individualized education and transition plans that include goals that are standards-based, appropriate accommodations and modifications, and fair grading practices, and transition goals that are aligned with student needs.

Assessment (cont'd)

HLP6	Use student assessment data, analyze instructional practices, and make necessary adjustments that improve student outcomes.

After special education teachers develop instructional goals, they evaluate and make ongoing adjustments to students' instructional programs. Once instruction and other supports are designed and implemented, special education teachers have the skill to manage and engage in ongoing data collection using curriculum-based measures, informal classroom assessments, observations of student academic performance and behavior, self-assessment of classroom instruction, and discussions with key stakeholders (i.e., students, families, other professionals). Teachers study their practice to improve student learning, validate reasoned hypotheses about salient instructional features, and enhance instructional decision making. Effective teachers retain, reuse, and extend practices that improve student learning and adjust or discard those that do not.

Social/Emotional/Behavioral Practices

HLP7	Establish a consistent, organized, and respectful learning environment.

To build and foster positive relationships, teachers should establish age-appropriate and culturally responsive expectations, routines, and procedures within their classrooms that are positively stated and explicitly taught and practiced across the school year. When students demonstrate mastery and follow established rules and routines, teachers should provide age-appropriate specific performance feedback in meaningful and caring ways. By establishing, following, and reinforcing expectations of all students within the classroom, teachers will reduce the potential for challenging behavior and increase student engagement. When establishing learning environments, teachers should build mutually respectful relationships with students and engage them in setting the classroom climate (e.g., rules and routines); be respectful; and value ethnic, cultural, contextual, and linguistic diversity to foster student engagement across learning environments.

Social/Emotional/Behavioral Practices (cont'd)

HLP8	Provide positive and constructive feedback to guide students' learning and behavior.

The purpose of feedback is to guide student learning and behavior and increase student motivation, engagement, and independence, leading to improved student learning and behavior. Effective feedback must be strategically delivered and goal directed; feedback is most effective when the learner has a goal and the feedback informs the learner regarding areas needing improvement and ways to improve performance. Feedback may be verbal, nonverbal, or written, and should be timely, contingent, genuine, meaningful, age appropriate, and at rates commensurate with task and phase of learning (i.e., acquisition, fluency, maintenance). Teachers should provide ongoing feedback until learners reach their established learning goals.

HLP9	Teach social behaviors.

Teachers should explicitly teach appropriate interpersonal skills, including communication, and self-management, aligning lessons with classroom and schoolwide expectations for student behavior. Prior to teaching, teachers should determine the nature of the social skill challenge. If students do not know how to perform a targeted social skill, direct social skill instruction should be provided until mastery is achieved. If students display performance problems, the appropriate social skill should initially be taught, then emphasis should shift to prompting the student to use the skill and ensuring the "appropriate" behavior accesses the same or a similar outcome (i.e., is reinforcing to the student) as the problem behavior.

HLP10	Conduct functional behavioral assessments to develop individual student behavior support plans.

Creating individual behavior plans is a central role of all special educators. Key to successful plans is to conduct a functional behavioral assessment (FBA) any time behavior is chronic, intense, or impedes learning. A comprehensive FBA results in a hypothesis about the function of the student's problem behavior. Once the function is determined, a behavior intervention plan is developed that (a) teaches the student a pro-social replacement behavior that will serve the same or similar function, (b) alters the environment to make the replacement behavior more efficient and effective than the problem behavior, (c) alters the environment to no longer allow the problem behavior to access the previous outcome, and (d) includes ongoing data collection to monitor progress.

Instruction

HLP11	Identify and prioritize long- and short-term learning goals.

Teachers prioritize what is most important for students to learn by providing meaningful access to and success in the general education and other contextually relevant curricula. Teachers use grade-level standards, assessment data and learning progressions, students' prior knowledge, and IEP goals and benchmarks to make decisions about what is most crucial to emphasize, and develop long- and short-term goals accordingly. They understand essential curriculum components, identify essential prerequisites and foundations, and assess student performance in relation to these components.

HLP12	Systematically design instruction toward a specific learning goal.

Teachers help students to develop important concepts and skills that provide the foundation for more complex learning. Teachers sequence lessons that build on each other and make connections explicit, in both planning and delivery. They activate students' prior knowledge and show how each lesson "fits" with previous ones. Planning involves careful consideration of learning goals, what is involved in reaching the goals, and allocating time accordingly. Ongoing changes (e.g., pacing, examples) occur throughout the sequence based on student performance.

HLP13	Adapt curriculum tasks and materials for specific learning goals.

Teachers assess individual student needs and adapt curriculum materials and tasks so that students can meet instructional goals. Teachers select materials and tasks based on student needs; use relevant technology; and make modifications by highlighting relevant information, changing task directions, and decreasing amounts of material. Teachers make strategic decisions on content coverage (i.e., essential curriculum elements), meaningfulness of tasks to meet stated goals, and criteria for student success.

Instruction (cont'd)

HLP14	Teach cognitive and metacognitive strategies to support learning and independence.

Teachers explicitly teach cognitive and metacognitive processing strategies to support memory, attention, and self-regulation of learning. Learning involves not only understanding content but also using cognitive processes to solve problems, regulate attention, organize thoughts and materials, and monitor one's own thinking. Self-regulation and metacognitive strategy instruction is integrated into lessons on academic content through modeling and explicit instruction. Students learn to monitor and evaluate their performance in relation to explicit goals and make necessary adjustments to improve learning.

HLP15	Provide scaffolded supports.

Scaffolded supports provide temporary assistance to students so they can successfully complete tasks that they cannot yet do independently and with a high rate of success. Teachers select powerful visual, verbal, and written supports; carefully calibrate them to students' performance and understanding in relation to learning tasks; use them flexibly; evaluate their effectiveness; and gradually remove them once they are no longer needed. Some supports are planned prior to lessons and some are provided responsively during instruction.

HLP16	Use explicit instruction.

Teachers make content, skills, and concepts explicit by showing and telling students what to do or think while solving problems, enacting strategies, completing tasks, and classifying concepts. Teachers use explicit instruction when students are learning new material and complex concepts and skills. They strategically choose examples and non-examples and language to facilitate student understanding, anticipate common misconceptions, highlight essential content, and remove distracting information. They model and scaffold steps or processes needed to understand content and concepts, apply skills, and complete tasks successfully and independently.

Instruction (cont'd)

HLP17	Use flexible grouping.

Teachers assign students to homogeneous and heterogeneous groups based on explicit learning goals, monitor peer interactions, and provide positive and corrective feedback to support productive learning. Teachers use small learning groups to accommodate learning differences, promote in-depth academic-related interactions, and teach students to work collaboratively. They choose tasks that require collaboration, issue directives that promote productive and autonomous group interactions, and embed strategies that maximize learning opportunities and equalize participation. Teachers promote simultaneous interactions, use procedures to hold students accountable for collective and individual learning, and monitor and sustain group performance through proximity and positive feedback.

HLP18	Use strategies to promote active student engagement.

Teachers use a variety of instructional strategies that result in active student responding. Active student engagement is critical to academic success. Teachers must initially build positive student–teacher relationships to foster engagement and motivate reluctant learners. They promote engagement by connecting learning to students' lives (e. g., knowing students' academic and cultural backgrounds) and using a variety of teacher-led (e.g., choral responding and response cards), peer-assisted (e. g., cooperative learning and peer tutoring), student-regulated (e.g., self-management), and technology-supported strategies shown empirically to increase student engagement. They monitor student engagement and provide positive and constructive feedback to sustain performance.

HLP19	Use assistive and instructional technologies.

Teachers select and implement assistive and instructional technologies to support the needs of students with disabilities. They select and use augmentative and alternative communication devices and assistive and instructional technology products to promote student learning and independence. They evaluate new technology options given student needs; make informed instructional decisions grounded in evidence, professional wisdom, and students' IEP goals; and advocate for administrative support in technology implementation. Teachers use the universal design for learning (UDL) framework to select, design, implement, and evaluate important student outcomes.

Instruction (cont'd)

HLP20	Provide intensive instruction.

Teachers match the intensity of instruction to the intensity of the student's learning and behavioral challenges. Intensive instruction involves working with students with similar needs on a small number of high priority, clearly defined skills or concepts critical to academic success. Teachers group students based on common learning needs; clearly define learning goals; and use systematic, explicit, and well-paced instruction. They frequently monitor students' progress and adjust their instruction accordingly. Within intensive instruction, students have many opportunities to respond and receive immediate, corrective feedback with teachers and peers to practice what they are learning.

HLP21	Teach students to maintain and generalize new learning across time and settings.

Effective teachers use specific techniques to teach students to generalize and maintain newly acquired knowledge and skills. Using numerous examples in designing and delivering instruction requires students to apply what they have learned in other settings. Educators promote maintenance by systematically using schedules of reinforcement, providing frequent material reviews, and teaching skills that are reinforced by the natural environment beyond the classroom. Students learn to use new knowledge and skills in places and situations other than the original learning environment and maintain their use in the absence of ongoing instruction.

HLP22	Provide positive and constructive feedback to guide students' learning and behavior.

The purpose of feedback is to guide student learning and behavior and increase student motivation, engagement, and independence, leading to improved student learning and behavior. Effective feedback must be strategically delivered and goal directed; feedback is most effective when the learner has a goal and the feedback informs the learner regarding areas needing improvement and ways to improve performance. Feedback may be verbal, nonverbal, or written, and should be timely, contingent, genuine, meaningful, age appropriate, and at rates commensurate with task and phase of learning (i.e., acquisition, fluency, maintenance). Teachers should provide ongoing feedback until learners reach their established learning goals.

References

Linn, D., & Hemmer, L. (2011). English language learner disproportionality in special education: Implications for the scholar-practitioner. *Journal of Educational Research and Practice, 1*, 70–80. doi:10.5590/JERAP.2011.01.1.06

U.S. Department of Education (2016). *Racial and ethnic disparities in special education.* Washington, DC: Office of Special Education and Rehabilitation. Retrieved from http://www2.ed.gov/programs/osepidea/618-data/LEA-racial-ethnic-disparities-tables/disproportionality-analysis-by-state-analysis-category.pdf

Zhang, D., & Katsiyannis, A. (2002). Minority representation in special education: A persistent challenge. *Remedial & Special Education, 23,* 180–187. doi:10.1177/07419325020230030601

Research Syntheses: Collaboration High-Leverage Practices

Effective special education teachers collaborate with a wide range of professionals, families and caregivers to assure that educational programs and related services are effectively designed and implemented to meet the needs of each student with a disability. Collaboration allows for varied expertise and perspectives about a student to be shared among those responsible for the student's learning and well-being. This collective expertise provides collaborators with a more comprehensive understanding of each student's needs, which can be used to more effectively plan and implement instruction and services.

Teachers use respectful and effective communication skills as they collaborate with others, considering the background, socioeconomic status, culture, and language of the families and the professionals with whom they work. Collaborative activities should be focused on (a) designing each student's instructional program to meet clearly specified outcomes and (b) collecting data and monitoring progress toward these outcomes. Effective and purposeful collaboration should enlist support from district and school leaders, who can foster a collective commitment to collaboration, provide professional learning experiences to increase team members' collaborative skills, and create schedules that support different forms of ongoing collaboration (e.g., individualized education program [IEP] teams, co-teachers, teachers–families, teachers–paraprofessionals).

HLP1	**Collaborate with professionals to increase student success.**

Collaboration with general education teachers, paraprofessionals, and support staff is necessary to support students' learning toward measurable outcomes and to facilitate students' social and emotional well-being across all school environments and instructional settings (e.g., co-taught). Collaboration with individuals or teams requires the use of effective collaboration behaviors (e.g., sharing ideas, active listening, questioning, planning, problem solving, negotiating) to develop and adjust instructional or behavioral plans based on student data, and the coordination of expectations, responsibilities, and resources to maximize student learning.

Collaboration is broadly recommended in special education for accomplishing a wide range of goals, including determining eligibility for services, delivering instruction, ensuring support through paraprofessionals, and resolving student and programmatic issues (see Burns, Vanderwood, & Ruby, 2005). However, collaboration is ethereal in that it is never an end in itself, instead operating as a culture or a means through which any goal can be reached. Collaboration often is indirectly fostered among members of a school work group by arranging time for participants to meet face-to-face, guiding them through the development of positive professional relationships, establishing explicit and implicit procedures for working together, and teaching them about school programs that rely on collaborative inter- actions (e.g., teams, co-teaching). Collabor- ation is not explicitly mandated in the Individuals With Disabilities Education Act (IDEA), nor is it generally part of formal policies related to educating students with disabilities, but the requirements of the law and established school practices strongly infer that it is through collaboration that the effective education of students with disabilities is achieved.

Asked to define *collaboration*, a typical response is "working together." However, a nuanced understanding suggests that collaboration is more about how individuals share their work, and it is characterized by voluntariness, mutual goals, parity, shared responsibility for critical decisions, joint accountability for outcomes, and shared resources (Friend & Cook, 2017). It is also developmental, growing over time as participants increase their trust of one another and create a sense of professional community. It is not surprising that research on collaboration is constrained by its elusive nature, by its innumerable applications, and by the number of variables that contribute to its existence.

Research Support

Research related to collaboration has consisted largely of anecdotal reports and surveys of individuals' perceptions about their collaborative experiences, including the importance of administrative support and the effect on student outcomes, often seasoned with advice for implementing collaborative strategies and exhortations about their importance. However, a handful of studies have examined collaboration with a more precise lens; these can be grouped into three categories: (a) those that broadly analyze the relationship between the presence of collaboration and student outcomes, (b) those that consider the effect of specific collaborative school structures, and (c) those that investigate specific components of collaboration.

Researchers have for many years studied schools in which students with disabilities (usually those with learning disabilities, other health impairment/ADHD, or autism spectrum disorder) outperform similar students in other locales, seeking common characteristics that contribute to their success. Collaborative culture or high value on collaboration is a typical finding in these studies (e.g., Caron & McLaughlin, 2002; Huberman, Navo, & Parrish, 2012). Attention has turned recently to analyzing whether specific aspects of collaboration are associated with such positive results. For example, in a study that included more than 9,000 teacher observations over 2 years as well as administrative and student data, Ronfeldt, Farmer, McQueen, and Grissom (2015)–accounting for factors that might lead to spurious correlational associations–found that teachers participating more frequently and with

Communication skills are key building blocks for collaboration.

more satisfaction in team activities, especially those related to assessments, produced relatively higher student achievement than teachers with less frequent and less satisfying team interactions. Ronfeldt et al. concluded that a causal relationship exists between collaboration and student outcomes.

The two most common school structures presumed to rely on collaboration are co-teaching and teams. Co-teaching research generally has found strong support among teachers but mixed results for students (Murawski & Swanson, 2001; Scruggs, Mastropieri, & McDuffie, 2007). The most recent examination of the co-teaching research literature, an analysis of six co-teaching and inclusion research syntheses, concluded that when general educators

and special educators work closely to coordinate the delivery of curriculum and have resources such as time to plan, small positive effects on student academic outcomes are achieved (Solis, Vaughn, Swanson, & McCulley, 2012). A related study supported this conclusion, finding that elementary-age students with disabilities in co-taught classes made significant educational progress while those in separate special education classroom settings did not, the gap between the two groups widening across time (Tremblay, 2013).

Similarly, collaboration has been associated with positive outcomes on student-centered problem-solving teams (Sheridan et al., 2004). However, much of the research on teams has focused on their general characteristics, including the importance of member interdependence, individual accountability, satisfaction of member needs, clarity of roles and expectations, and diversity of expertise among team members (e.g., Park, Henkin, & Egley, 2005). Other variables considered include teacher empowerment (Rafoth & Foriska, 2006) and the positive association of professional familiarity with team effectiveness (Killumets, D'Innocenzo, Maynard, & Mathieu, 2015).

Communication skills are key building blocks for collaboration; participants' verbal and nonverbal skills largely define whether collaboration can occur. For example, relatively equal amounts of talk by participants, the use of words that suggest instead of advise, and the interplay of who structures the flow of the interaction and who influences its content promote a perception of collaboration (Erchul et al., 1999). An additional element of collaboration is trust, and qualitative research indicates that trust is a facilitator for collaboration because it enables participants to communicate clearly, even on topics that might be considered sensitive (Hallam, Smith, Hite, Hite, & Wilcox, 2015).

Conclusion

Collaboration is intuitively appealing but extraordinarily challenging to study using rigorous research designs. Even though some evidence exists to demonstrate the effectiveness of collaboration, much of that evidence consists of case studies, program evaluation, and qualitative research. At this time, only limited rigorous empirical evidence guides practitioners regarding the criteria for assessing the quality of collaboration or for determining whether collaboration has a direct and positive effect on outcomes for students with disabilities.

HLP2	Organize and facilitate effective meetings with professionals and families.

Teachers lead and participate in a range of meetings (e.g., meetings with families, individualized education program [IEP] teams, individualized family services plan [IFSP] teams, instructional planning) with the purpose of identifying clear, measurable student outcomes and developing instructional and behavioral plans that support these outcomes. They develop a meeting agenda, allocate time to meet the goals of the agenda, and lead in ways that encourage consensus building through positive verbal and nonverbal communication, encouraging the sharing of multiple perspectives, demonstrating active listening, and soliciting feedback.

Special education teachers typically organize, schedule, and lead a variety of meetings, including annual IEP meetings as well as ongoing collaborative meetings essential to instructional planning and progress monitoring. IEP meetings involve both parents and professionals (e.g., general education teachers, fellow special education teachers, reading specialists, curriculum specialists, principals, other administrators, outside consultants), as well as students with disabilities. IDEA requires that parents be given opportunities for full participation in the development of the IEP. The way in which the IEP meeting is organized and facilitated should ensure that the family is an equal partner in the development of an appropriate education for the child.

Special education teachers need to facilitate meetings so they run smoothly, involve others as equal participants, and accomplish the goals of the meeting. These tasks require communicating effectively with others, being able discuss aspects of the individual child's program (e.g., explain the rationale behind behavior intervention plans, describe effective practices), and facilitating consensus among all involved. The partnership principles of equality, choice, voice, reciprocity, praxis, and reflection aid in the development of effective communication skills (Knight, 2007). Using these principles requires specific skills, which may be developed with diligent practice. It may be helpful to solicit feedback from a mentor or colleague as well as team members to improve one's communication and facilitation skills.

The Council for Exceptional Children's special education Code of Ethics (2015) includes the following principles relating to organizing and facilitating effective meetings:

- Practicing collegially with others who are providing services to individuals with exceptionalities.

- Developing relationships with families based on mutual respect and actively involving families and individuals with exceptionalities in educational decision making. (p. 7)

Research and Policy Support

Collaboration—when teachers work together to diagnose what they need to do, plan and teach interventions, and evaluate their effectiveness—has shown a strong effect size of 0.93 on student achievement (DuFour, 2007; Hattie, 2008). Effective meetings are facilitated by building trust (Fullan, 2008; Reina & Reina, 2006), communicating clearly (Patterson, Grenny, McMillan, & Switzler, 2012), listening carefully to others' concerns and opinions (Covey, 2004; Knight, 2007; Patterson et al., 2012), and holding a belief in equality as shown through genuine respect for others (Knight, 2007). In addition to interactions with colleagues, Blue-Banning, Summers, Frankland, Nelson, and Beegle (2004) recommended the aforementioned attitudes and behaviors to promote positive relationships with parents. Further, the association Learning Forward has recommended using problem-solving protocols for teams and individuals who

Collaboration—when teachers work together to diagnose what they need to do, plan and teach interventions, and evaluate their effectiveness—has shown a strong effect size of 0.93 on student achievement. Effective meetings are facilitated by building trust, communicating clearly, listening carefully to others' concerns and opinions

face frustrating situations (Killion, Harrison, Bryan, & Clifton, 2012). Fortunately, researchers have found that these communication behaviors can be learned (Patterson et al., 2012).

Meeting agendas should be planned in a way that invites the sharing of multiple perspectives, involves active listening, and encourages consensus building, while maintaining efficiency. Agendas for formal meetings should be developed and shared in advance; the meeting should be scheduled for an appropriate amount of time given meeting goals and participants invited with sufficient advance notice.

In addition, case law supports the notion that the IEP is the centerpiece of IDEA law and that the student's parents or guardians are considered full and equal partners in its development. Teachers need to understand what is to be accomplished at IEP meetings and to ensure that all requirements are met. It is not appropriate to come to the meeting with a completed IEP, and special educators need to be sure parents have meaningful opportunities to contribute. For example, a translator will need to be available if the parent does not speak English. It also may be important to send information to parents prior to the IEP meeting, so they understand the purpose of the meeting and understand that they will be given opportunities share information about their child and to make suggestions. Sample IEP agendas are available online (e.g., www.PACER.org) and may be provided by a state's department of education or a local director of special education.

Finally, meetings will be more productive if there is trust among participants. Teachers should consider taking steps before meetings to build relationships with professionals and families on an ongoing basis (Billingsley, Brownell, Israel, & Kamman, 2013). At the start of the school year, effective special educators communicate with families via phone, e-mail, or notes home with positive messages about individual children and their accomplishments. At IEP team meetings, special educators should communicate the value of all participants' input, allow time for introductions and celebrations, and discuss meeting outcomes and goals. It is often helpful to briefly discuss ground rules for the meeting (e.g., expectations, norms, community principles). Team members' satisfaction with the process and outcomes of meetings can be improved with goal setting and ongoing feedback, which is referred to as the *social acceptability* of meetings (Reinig, 2003). As special educators are primary communicators in the school regarding students with disabilities, they also should serve as models of respectful communication by using person-first language.

Conclusion

There are two ways to consider the research available on meetings with professionals and families: effectiveness and social acceptability. Although little research is available about organizing and facilitating meetings, evidence does suggest the importance of having clear meeting goals, establishing a meeting agenda, setting expectations, using active listening, and encouraging genuine communication. Research on social acceptability is typically focused on team members' satisfaction (Reinig, 2003). Employing a partnership approach with professionals and parents makes gathering valuable input possible, and makes messages more receivable and meetings more effective (Knight, 2007).

HLP3	**Collaborate with families to support student learning and secure needed services.**

Teachers collaborate with families about individual children's needs, goals, programs, and progress over time and ensure families are informed about their rights as well as about special education processes (e.g., IEPs, IFSPs). Teachers should respectfully and effectively communicate considering the background, socioeconomic status, language, culture, and priorities of the family. Teachers advocate for resources to help students meet instructional, behavioral, social, and transition goals. In building positive relationships with students, teachers encourage students to self-advocate, with the goal of fostering self-determination over time. Teachers also work with families to self-advocate and support their children's learning.

The importance of collaborating with families to promote participation in educational decision making has been identified as one of the key principles of IDEA (H. R. Turnbull, Stowe, & Huerta, 2007).

IDEA provides for specific rights that enable parents to participate as equal members of the IEP team and to be involved in evaluation, placement, and special education and related service decisions. For families to take on such roles and responsibilities, collaboration between professionals and families is necessary. Using effective partnership strategies has been identified as a necessary element of building collaborative relationships.

Family-professional partnerships have been defined as

> a relationship in which families (not just parents) and professionals agree to build on each other's expertise and resources, as appropriate, for the purpose of making and implementing decisions that will directly benefit students and indirectly benefit other family members and professionals. (A. P. Turnbull, Turnbill, Erwin, Soodak, & Shogren, 2015, p. 161)

Seven principles of effective partnerships have been identified in the literature (see A. P. Turnbull et al., 2015):

- Communication: Teachers and families communicate openly and honestly in a medium that is comfortable for the family.

- Professional competence: Teachers are highly qualified in the area in which they work, continue to learn and grow, and have and communicate high expectations for students and families.

- Respect. Teachers treat families with dignity, honor cultural diversity, and affirm strengths.

- Commitment: Teachers are available, consistent, and go above and beyond what is expected of them.

- Equality; Teachers recognize the strengths of every member of a team, share power with families, and focus on working together with families.

- Advocacy: Teachers focus on getting to the best solution for the student in partnership with the family.

- Trust: Teachers are reliable and act in the best interest of the student, sharing their vision and actions with the family.

Research Support

Researchers have examined issues related to the process of establishing family-professional partnerships and the effect of these partnerships on child and family outcomes. This body of research has used multiple methods (i.e., qualitative, quantitative, meta-analytic) to descriptively and empirically examine the effect of collaboration. Several studies have examined the relationship between family-professional partnerships and family outcomes, finding that parents report less stress, greater family quality of life, and greater satisfaction with education and related services when partnerships are stronger (Burke & Hodapp, 2014; Eskow, Chasson, Mitchell, & Summers, 2015; Neece, Kraemer, & Blacher, 2009; Shogren, McCart, Lyon, & Sailor, 2015).

Researchers also have found that when educators use the principles of effective partnerships, this influences families' perceptions of and engagement in education planning. For example, communicating information in a respectful way—particularly by sharing information about testing results and educational progress using accessible and family-friendly language and mediums (i.e., videos, family portfolios)—leads to greater feelings of parent empowerment (Childre & Chambers, 2005; Klein et al., 2011; Meadan, Thompson, et al., 2009; Thompson, Meadan, Fansler, Alber, & Balogh, 2007). Addressing issues of cultural diversity is also essential (Kalyanpur, Harry, & Skrtic, 2000; Shogren, 2012; Valenzuela & Martin, 2005); using cultural navigators or parent or school liaisons who serve as brokers to promote respect and communication between families and educators of differing cultural backgrounds leads to increased parent involvement and families perceiving educators as trustworthy and advocating for child outcomes (Balcazar et al., 2012; Hardin, Mereoiu, Hung, & Roach-Scott, 2009; Howland, Anderson, Smiley, & Abbott, 2006).

There is a significant body of research that suggests that families, with support from teachers and related service professionals, learn and implement various teaching strategies in the home. For example, with regard to support-

> *When teachers and families effectively collaborate to set goals, children make more gains.*

ing positive behavior (and eliminating challenging behavior) in the home, significant child- and family-level outcomes result when families are provided with culturally responsive training and support that promotes feelings of equality and trust in professionals (Kim, Sheridan, Kwon, & Koziol, 2013; Lucyshyn et al., 2007; McCormick, Cappella, O'Connor, & McClowry, 2013; McLaughlin, Denney, Snyder, & Welsh, 2012; Meadan, Ostrosky, Zaghlawan, & Yu, 2009). Families also play an important role in teaching self-determination skills, during early childhood (Brotherson, Cook, Erwin, & Weigel, 2008; Cook, Brotherson, Weigel-Garrey, & Mize, 1996; Erwin et al., 2009; Palmer et al., in press; Summers et al., 2014) and across the lifespan (Shogren, 2012; Shogren, Garnier Villarreal, Dowsett, & Little, 2016; Zhang, 2005). Further, when teachers and families effectively collaborate to set goals, children make more gains in the attainment of goals, which suggests the importance of

partnerships in influencing child outcomes (Childre & Chambers, 2005; Palmer et al., in press). Finally, engaging families in transition planning has the potential to affect students' postschool outcomes (Test et al., 2009), and increasing family knowledge influences family expectations for postschool outcomes (Young, Morgan, Callow-Heusser, & Lindstrom, 2016), which can lead to greater advocacy on the part of families and young adults with disabilities, particularly related to employment (Francis, Gross, Turnbull, & Turnbull, 2013; Francis, Gross, Turnbull, & Parent-Johnson, 2013).

Conclusion

A diverse body of research suggests the positive effect of building collaborative relationships between educators and families using effective partnership principles. These effects include not only improvements in teacher–family relationships and increases in shared decision making, but also child-level and family-level effects. A clear set of principles that define effective partnerships have emerged from research which emphasize creating trusting partnerships through communication, professional competence, respect, commitment, equality, and advocacy. In implementing these principles, it is essential to honor and respect cultural diversity and differing communication styles and preferences.

References

Balcazar, F. E., Taylor-Ritzler, T., Dimpfl, S., Portillo-Peña, N., Guzman, A., Schiff, R., & Murvay, M. (2012). Improving the transition outcomes of low-income minority youth with disabilities. *Exceptionality, 20*, 114–132. doi:10.1080/09362835.2012.670599

Billingsley, B. S., Brownell, M. T., Israel, M., & Kamman, M. L. (2013). *A survival guide for new special educators.* San Franciso, CA: Jossey-Bass.

Blue-Banning, M., Summers, J. A., Frankland, H. C., Nelson, L. L., & Beegle, G. (2004). Dimensions of family and professional partnerships: Constructive guidelines for collaboration. *Exceptional Children, 70,* 167–184. doi:10.1177/001440290407000203

Burns, M. K., Vanderwood, M. L., & Ruby, S. (2005). Evaluating the readiness of pre-referral intervention teams for use in a problem solving model. *School Psychology Quarterly, 20,* 89–105. doi:10.1521/scpq.20.1.89.64192

Brotherson, M. J., Cook, C. C., Erwin, E. E., & Weigel, C. J. (2008). Understanding self-determination and families of young children with disabilities in home environments. *Journal of Early Intervention, 31,* 22–43. doi:10.1177/1053815108324445

Burke, M. M., & Hodapp, R. M. (2014). Relating stress of mothers of children with developmental disabilities to family–school partnerships. *Intellectual and Developmental Disabilities, 52,* 13–23. doi:10.1352/1934-9556-52.1.13

Caron, E.A. & McLaughlin, M.J. (2002). Indicators of Beacons of Excellence schools: What do they tell us about collaborative practices? *Journal of Educational and Psychological Consultation, 13,* 285–313. doi:10.1207/S1532768XJEPC1304_03

Childre, A., & Chambers, C. R. (2005). Family perceptions of student centered planning and IEP meetings. *Education and Training in Developmental Disabilities, 40,* 217–233.

Cook, C. C., Brotherson, M. J., Weigel-Garrey, C., & Mize, I. (1996). Homes to support the self-determination of children. In D. J. Sands & M. L. Wehmeyer (Eds.), *Self-determination across the lifespan: Independence and choice for people with disabilities* (pp. 91–110). Baltimore, MD: Brookes.

Council for Exceptional Children. (2015). *What every special educator must know: Professional ethics & standards* (7th ed.). Arlington, VA: Author.

Covey, S. (2004). *The 7 habits of highly effective people: Powerful lessons in personal change.* New York, NY: Simon & Schuster.

DuFour, R. (2007). Professional learning communities: A bandwagon, an idea worth considering, or our best hope for high levels of learning? *Middle School Journal, 39*(1), 4–8. doi:10.1080/00940771.2007.11461607

Erchul, W. P., Sheridan, S. M., Ryan, D. A., Grissom, P. F., Killough, C. E., & Mettler, D. W. (1999). Patterns of relational communication in conjoint behavioral consultation. *School Psychology Quarterly, 14*, 121-147. doi:10.1037/h0089001

Erwin, E. J., Brotherson, M. J., Palmer, S. B., Cook, C. C., Weigel, C. J., & Summers, J. A. (2009). How to promote self-determination for young children with disabilities: Evidence-based strategies for early childhood practitioners and families. *Young Exceptional Children, 12*, 27-37.

Eskow, K., Chasson, G., Mitchell, R., & Summers, J. A. (2015). Association between parent-teacher partnership satisfaction and outcomes for children and families with autism. Manuscript submitted for publication.

Francis, G. L., Gross, J. M. S., Turnbull, A. P., & Turnbull, H. R. (2013). The Family Employment Awareness Training (FEAT): A mixed-method follow-up. *Journal of Vocational Rehabilitation, 39*, 167-181.

Francis, G. L., Gross, J. M. S., Turnbull, H. R., & Parent-Johnson, W. (2013). Evaluating the effectiveness of the Family Employment Awareness Training in Kansas: A pilot study. *Research and Practice for Persons with Severe Disabilities, 38*, 1-14. doi:10.2511/027494813807046953

Friend, M., & Cook, L. (2017). *Interactions: Collaboration skills for school professionals* (8th ed.). Upper Saddle River, NJ: Pearson.

Fullan, M. (2008). *The six secrets of change: What the best leaders do to help their organizations survive and thrive*. San Francisco, CA: Jossey-Bass.

Hallam, P. R., Smith, H. R., Hite, J. M., Hite, S. J., & Wilcox, B. R. (2015). Trust and collaboration in PLC teams: Teacher relationships, principal support, and collaborative benefits. *NASSP Bulletin, 99*, 193-216. doi:10.1177/0192636515602330

Hardin, B. J., Mereoiu, M., Hung, H. F., & Roach-Scott, M. (2009). Investigating parent and professional perspectives concerning special education services for preschool Latino children. *Early Childhood Education Journal, 37*, 93-102. doi:10.1007/s10643-009-0336-x

Hattie, J. (2008). *Visible learning: A synthesis of over 800 meta-analyses relating to achievement*. New York, NY: Routledge.

Howland, A., Anderson, J. A., Smiley, A. D., & Abbott, D. J. (2006). School liaisons: Bridging the gap between home and school. *School Community Journal, 16*, 47-68.

Huberman, M., Navo, M., & Parrish, T. (2012). Effective practices in high performing districts serving students in special education. *Journal of Special Education Leadership, 25*(2), 59-71.

Kalyanpur, M., Harry, B., & Skrtic, T. (2000). Equity and advocacy expectations of culturally diverse families' participation in special education. *International Journal of Disability, Development, and Education, 47*, 119-136. doi:10.1080/713671106

Killion, J., Harrison, C., Bryan, C., & Clifton, H. (2012). *Coaching matters*. Oxford, OH: Learning Forward.

Killumets, E., D'Innocenzo, L., Maynard, M. T., & Mathieu, J. E. (2015). A multilevel examination of the impact of team interpersonal processes. *Small Group Research, 46*, 227–259. doi:10.1177/1046496415573631

Kim, E. M., Sheridan, S. M., Kwon, K., & Koziol, N. (2013). Parent beliefs and children's social-behavioral functioning: The mediating role of parent–teacher relationships. *Journal of School Psychology, 51*, 175–185. doi:10.1016/j.jsp.2013.01.003

Klein, S., Wynn, K., Ray, L., Demeriez, L., LaBerge, P., Pei, J., & Pierre, C. S. (2011). Information sharing during diagnostic assessments: What is relevant for parents? *Physical & Occupational Therapy in Pediatric, 31*, 120–132. doi:10.3109/01942638.2010.523450

Knight, J. (2007). *Instructional coaching: A partnership approach to improving instruction*. Thousand Oaks, CA: Corwin Press.

Lucyshyn, J. M., Albin, R. W., Horner, R. H., Mann, J. C., Mann, J. A., & Wadsworth, G. (2007). Family implementation of positive behavior support for a child with autism: Longitudinal, single-case, experimental, and descriptive replication and extension. *Journal of Positive Behavior Interventions, 9*, 131–150. doi:10.1177/10983007070090030201

McCormick, M. P., Cappella, E., O'Connor, E. E., & McClowry, S. G. (2013). Parent involvement, emotional support, and behavior problems: An ecological approach. *The Elementary School Journal, 114*, 276–300. doi:10.1086/673200

McLaughlin, T. W., Denney, M. K., Snyder, P. A., & Welsh, J. L. (2012). Behavioral support interventions implemented by families of young children: Examination of contextual fit. *Journal of Positive Behavior Interventions, 14*, 87–97. doi:10.1177/1098300711411305

Meadan, H., Ostrosky, M. M., Zaghlawan, H. Y., & Yu, S. Y. (2009). Promoting the social and communicative behavior of young children with autism spectrum disorders: A review of parent-implemented intervention studies. *Topics in Early Childhood Special Education, 29*, 90–104. doi:10.1177/0271121409337950

Meadan, H., Thompson, J. R., Hagiwara, M., Herold, J., Hoekstra, S., & Manser, S. (2009). Evaluating the acceptability and effectiveness of family assessment portfolios. *Education and Training in Developmental Disabilities, 44*, 421–430.

Murawski, W., & Swanson, H. (2001). A meta-analysis of co-teaching research: Where are the data? *Remedial and Special Education, 22*, 258–267. doi:10.1177/074193250102200501

Neece, C. L., Kraemer, B. R., & Blacher, J. (2009). Transition satisfaction and family well being among parents of young adults with severe intellectual disability. *Intellectual and Developmental Disabilities, 47*, 31–43. doi:10.1352/2009.47:31-43

Palmer, S. B., Summers, J. A., Brotherson, M. J., Erwin, E. J., Maude, S. P., Haines, S. J., & Stroup-Rentier, V. L. (in press). Foundations for self-determination in early childhood intervention: Fidelity, feasibility, and outcomes. *Journal of Early Intervention.*

Park, S., Henkin, A. B., & Egley, R. (2005). Teacher team commitment, teamwork and trust: Exploring associations. *Journal of Educational Administration, 43,* 462–479. doi:10.1108/09578230510615233

Patterson, K., Grenny, J., McMillan, R., & Switzler, A. (2012). *Crucial conversations.* New York, NY: McGraw-Hill.

Rafoth, M. A., & Foriska, T. (2006). Administrator participation in promoting effective problem-solving teams. *Remedial and Special Education, 27,* 130–135. doi:10.1177/07419325060270030101

Reina, D. S., & Reina, M. L. (2006). *Trust and betrayal in the workplace: Building effective relationships in your organization.* (2nd ed.) San Francisco, CA: Berrett-Koeler.

Reinig, B. A. (2003). Toward an understanding of satisfaction with the process and outcomes of teamwork. *Journal of Management Information Systems, 19,* 65–83.

Ronfeldt, M., Farmer, S. O., McQueen, K., & Grissom, J. A. (2015). Teacher collaboration in instructional teams and student achievement. *American Educational Research Journal, 52,* 475–514. doi:10.3102/0002831215585562

Scruggs, T. E., Mastropieri, M. A., & McDuffie, K. A. (2007). Co-teaching in inclusive classrooms: A metasynthesis of qualitative research. *Exceptional Children, 73,* 392–416. doi:10.1177/001440290707300401

Sheridan, S. M., Erchul, W. P., Brown, M. S., Dowd, S. E., Warnes, E. D., Marti, D. C., … Eagle, J. W. (2004). Perceptions of helpfulness in conjoint behavioral consultation: Congruence and agreement between teachers and parents. *School Psychology Quarterly, 19,* 121–140. doi:10.1521/scpq.19.2.121.33308

Shogren, K. A. (2012). Hispanic mothers' perceptions of self-determination. *Research and Practice for Persons with Severe Disabilities, 37,* 170–184. doi:10.2511/027494812804153561

Shogren, K. A., Garnier Villarreal, M., Dowsett, C., & Little, T. D. (2016). Exploring student, family, and school predictors of self-determination using NLTS2 data. *Career Development and Transition for Exceptional Individuals, 37,* 23–33. doi:10.1177/2165143414546685

Shogren, K. A., McCart, A., Lyon, K. J., & Sailor, W. (2015). All means all: Building knowledge for inclusive schoolwide transformation. *Research and Practice for Persons with Severe Disabilities, 40,* 173–191. doi:10.1177/1540796915586191

Solis, M., Vaughn, S., Swanson, E., & McCulley, L. (2012). Collaborative models of instruction: The empirical foundations of inclusion and co-teaching. *Psychology in the Schools, 49,* 498–510. doi:10.1002/pits.21606

Summers, J. A., Brotherson, M. J., Erwin, E. J., Maude, S. P., Palmer, S. B., Haines, S. J., ... Zheng, Y. Z. (2014). Family reflections on the foundations of self-determination in early childhood. *Inclusion, 2*, 175–194. doi:10.1352/2326-6988-2.03.175

Test, D. W., Mazzotti, V. L., Mustian, A. L., Fowler, C. H., Kortering, L., & Kohler, P. (2009). Evidence-based secondary transition predictors for improving postschool outcomes for students with disabilities. *Career Development for Exceptional Individuals, 32*, 160–181. doi:10.1177/0885728809346960

Thompson, J. R., Meadan, H., Fansler, K. W., Alber, S. B., & Balogh, P. A. (2007). Family assessment portfolios: A new way to jumpstart family/school collaboration. *TEACHING Exceptional Children, 39*(6), 19–25. doi:10.1177/004005990703900603

Tremblay, P. (2013). Comparative outcomes of two instructional models for students with learning disabilities: Inclusion with co-teaching and solo-taught special education. *Journal of Research in Special Educational Needs, 13*, 251–258. doi:10.1111/j.1471-3802.2012.01270.x

Turnbull, A. P., Turnbull, H. R., Erwin, E. E., Soodak, L. C., & Shogren, K. A. (2015). *Families, professionals, and exceptionality: Positive outcomes through partnership and trust* (7th ed.). Upper Saddle River, NJ: Merrill Prentice Hall.

Turnbill, H. R., Stowe, M. J., & Huerta, N. E. (2007). *Free appropriate public education: The law and students with disabilities* (7th ed.). Denver, CO: Love.

Valenzuela, R. L., & Martin, J. E. (2005). Self-directed IEP: Bridging values of diverse cultures and secondary education. *Career Development for Exceptional Individuals, 28*, 4–14. doi:10.1177/08857288050280010301

Young, J., Morgan, R. L., Callow-Heusser, C. A., & Lindstrom, L. (2016). The effects of parent training on knowledge of transition services for students with Disabilities. *Career Development and Transition for Exceptional Individuals, 39*, 79–87. doi:10.1177/2165143414549207

Zhang, D. (2005). Parent practices in facilitating self-determination skills: The influences of culture, socioeconomic status, and children's special education status. *Research and Practice for Persons with Severe Disabilities, 30*, 154–162. doi:10.2511/rpsd.30.3.154

Research Syntheses: Assessment High-Leverage Practices

Assessment plays a foundational role in special education. Students with disabilities are complex learners who have unique needs that exist alongside their strengths. Effective special education teachers have to fully understand those strengths and needs. Thus, these teachers are knowledgeable regarding assessment and are skilled in using and interpreting data. This includes formal, standardized assessments that are used in identifying students for special education services, developing students' individualized education programs (IEPs), and informing ongoing services. Formal assessments such as statewide exams also provide data regarding whether students with disabilities are achieving state content standards and how their academic progress compares to students without disabilities. Teachers are also knowledgeable about

and skillful in using informal assessments, such as those used to evaluate students' academic, behavioral, and functional strengths and needs. These assessments are used to develop students' IEPs, design and evaluate instruction, and monitor student progress. As reflective practitioners, special educators also continuously analyze the effect and effectiveness of their own instruction. Finally, these teachers are knowledgeable regarding how context, culture, language, and poverty might influence student performance; navigating conversations with families and other stakeholders; and choosing appropriate assessments given each student's profile. This is an especially important consideration, given the overrepresentation of culturally and linguistically diverse students and those from high poverty backgrounds in special education.

HLP4	Use multiple sources of information to develop a comprehensive understanding of a student's strengths and needs.

To develop a deep understanding of a student's learning needs, special educators compile a comprehensive learner profile through the use of a variety of assessment measures and other sources (e.g., information from parents, general educators, other stakeholders) that are sensitive to language and culture, to (a) analyze and describe students' strengths and needs and (b) analyze the school-based learning environments to determine potential supports and barriers to students' academic progress. Teachers should collect, aggregate, and interpret data from multiple sources (e.g., informal and formal observations, work samples, curriculum-based measures, functional behavior assessment [FBA], school files, analysis of curriculum, information from families, other data sources). This information is used to create an individualized profile of the student's strengths and needs.

Students with disabilities present a wide range of both strengths and needs, in a variety of areas (e.g., academic, social, emotional, adaptive and organizational, communication)—which must be understood in order to develop instruction specially designed to meet their needs. Their varied needs are most often the result of problems with attention, memory, language, emotional regulation, social regulation, and motivation due to repeated failure (Vaughn & Bos, 2014), and these underlying needs can interfere with their ability to achieve successful outcomes. There is evidence in the field of learning disabilities that performance on specific language and cognitive variables (e.g., phonological awareness, rapid letter naming, oral language skills, morphological awareness) can be used to identify students who need the most intensive, ongoing intervention (e.g., Al Otaiba & Fuchs, 2006; Fletcher et al., 2011; D. Fuchs et al., 2012). Further, response to instruction in reading and mathematics remains one of the strongest predictors of future performance (Katz, Stone, Carlisle, Corey, & Zeng, 2008; Vaughn, Linan-Thompson, & Hickman, 2003).

Environmental factors can play a role in student learning and behavior. Culture, language, and family poverty (along with teachers' response to these factors) can influence students' behavior and learning (Hammer et al., 2012; Judge & Bell, 2010; Samson & Lesaux, 2009). The instructional environment also can affect what students are learning. Well organized environments where student needs are supported positively influences students' learning and behavior (Murray & Greenburg, 2006).

Findings from research on individual learner characteristics, response to instruction, and the role of environmental factors in student learning suggest that special education teachers need to develop comprehensive learner profiles. These profiles should delineate students' strengths and needs, describe how culture and language might be influencing a student's performance, contain information about students' instructional environments, and show how students are responding to instruction. A comprehensive learner profile, continually revised based on instructional and behavioral data, is essential to develop, implement, evaluate, and revise instruction in ways that are sensitive to individual students' strengths and needs.

To develop a learner profile, special education teachers need to collect, over time, information from a variety of sources and synthesize that information in order to develop a comprehensive understanding of the student. These sources include but are not limited to:

- comprehensive, multidisciplinary assessments that produce information about cognitive and language variables;

- discussions with students' family members that provide information about students' interests and motivations and how they adapt to their home and community environment;

- curriculum-based measurement data that can be used to provide information about student progress in different curricular areas (Deno, Fuchs, Marston, & Shin, 2001);

- student interviews and surveys that generate data about students' interests in an academic area and their strategic approach to tasks (Montague, 1996);

- Inventories, classroom checklists, and student work samples that can be used to help teachers understand students' strengths and needs in an academic area (e.g., Leslie & Caldwell, 2015); and

- direct observation of classroom performance and behavior (e.g., functional behavioral assessment) that can be used to help teachers gather information such as how students perform a task and how students respond to different behavior and learning supports.

As special education teachers collect information, they need to look for and interpret patterns in the data, as this will help them to synthesize the information they are

collecting and to use the collected data for educational decision making. The synthesis of information can be used to develop a comprehensive profile of the individual student's strengths, needs, interests, and motivation in different areas, both academic and nonacademic. Understandings gained from these individual profiles can be used to communicate with professionals and parents in order to develop a team-based approach to the education of students with disabilities—one where information is used continually to design, evaluate, and revise instruction.

Research and Policy Support

The need to develop comprehensive learning profiles for students with disabilities is founded in research on assessment and effective special education teachers as well as the law governing the education of students with disabilities. Research on the limitations of standardized tests; the promise of formative, ongoing curricular and behavioral assessments; and the knowledge effective special education teachers have about students with disabilities suggests that teachers need rich information about students if they are going to respond effectively to their needs. In special education practice, the need for rich data—provided from the array of people involved in the student's education—arises from concerns about standardized, norm-referenced assessments. These assessments only provide a snapshot of how students perform in comparison to other students; they do not provide the specific information teachers need to develop interventions or assess their effectiveness (Caffrey, Fuchs, & Fuchs, 2008; Fuchs et al., 2008).

To be effective, special education teachers need data that helps them understand how students are learning and behaving in classrooms and schools. A robust research base exists that demonstrates the powerful role that ongoing collection of student achievement and behavioral data, or more formative assessments, can play in making instructional decisions about students (Stecker, Fuchs, & Fuchs, 2005). Teachers who frequently collect and analyze curriculum-relevant data are able to adapt and modify their instruction in ways that promote the learning of students with disabilities.

Studies of effective special education teachers have shown that they have a deep knowledge of students and how their students are learning in a particular area. These teachers are able to describe their students' academic, behavioral, and motivational needs in great detail (see Bishop, Brownell, Klingner, Leko, & Galman, 2010; Seo, Brownell, Bishop, & Dingle, 2008). They are careful observers of student behavior, provide skillful classroom management to support students' learning, and are able to engage in strategies that motivate their students to engage in instruction (Bishop et al, 2010; Brownell et al., 2014; Seo, 2006; Seo et al., 2008). Further, in two quantitative studies of special education teachers (Brownell et al., 2007, 2009), researchers showed that special education teachers with deep knowledge of content and of how students learn content are more effective in their ability to provide decoding and fluency instruction.

The Individuals With Disabilities Education Act (IDEA, 2006) requires that comprehensive evaluations of students with disabilities use a variety of assessment tools and strategies to develop an adequate picture of a student's strengths and needs (IDEA regulations, 2012, 34 C.F.R. § 300.304[b]; Center for Parent Information

and Resources, 2014). Further, this evaluation must be multidisciplinary (The National Dissemination Center for Children with Disabilities, n.d.). Parents, special education teachers, and other professionals (e.g., general education teachers, related service personnel) involved in the education of the student must contribute to the evaluation of the student.

Conclusion

Although both general and special education teachers need to develop assessment literacy and have an understanding of students' strengths, needs and interests, special education teachers are in the best position to develop a comprehensive learner profile for individual students. Special education teachers often have the most contact with students with disabilities, their families, and other professionals involved in the assessment of these students, and consequently are able to gather more comprehensive information about students from these different sources. In addition, the special education teacher is often the team member who provides the most intensive, small-group instruction to students with disabilities, and thus has an opportunity to know students in greater depth than a general education teacher might. To develop a comprehensive learner profile, effective special education teachers need to understand the different types of assessment tools available to them, and how to use those tools and the information generated from them to help the educational team design, implement, evaluate and revise programs that meet the individual needs of students with disabilities and allow them access to the general education curriculum.

> *Special education teachers with deep knowledge of content and of how students learn content are more effective in their ability to provide decoding and fluency instruction.*

HLP5	Interpret and communicate assessment information with stakeholders to collaboratively design and implement educational programs.

Teachers interpret assessment information for stakeholders (i.e., other professionals, families, students) and involve them in the assessment, goal development, and goal implementation process. Special educators must understand each assessment's purpose, help key stakeholders understand how culture and language influence interpretation of data generated, and use data to collaboratively develop and implement individualized education and transition plans that include goals that are standards-based, appropriate accommodations and modifications, and fair grading practices, and transition goals that are aligned with student needs.

IDEA recognizes the important role that a team plays in the evaluation of students and their ongoing education. One of the central components of providing services for students with disabilities is convening a team of stakeholders that includes key professionals and family members to collaboratively create an IEP (Council for Exceptional Children, n.d.). A high-quality IEP is the primary mechanism to individualize and assist students with disabilities in making progress. The special education teacher's role as a team member is to consider the student's strengths and needs based on assessment information and work collaboratively with the entire team to design an educational plan that, when implemented, will produce maximum benefit for the student. Because implementation and assessment of the educational plan are ongoing, special education teachers need to be able to interpret and communicate assessment results regularly with other teachers, staff, and families as part of the effort to monitor a student's response to instruction.

The first step in this process is to gather the assessment information and make it available to the IEP team, communicating the results in a format that is easily understood by all team members.

For some team members, assessment data may need to be interpreted with regard to its importance to developing goals, choosing appropriate accommodations and modifications, and identifying fair grading practices. Research indicates that parents often feel overwhelmed and anxious at IEP meetings, and family members have reported they understand none or only some of the information presented at the IEP meeting (Hammond, Ingalls, & Trussell, 2008). When parents are involved in the assessment process from the start they are better able to understand the purposes of the assessments and the results. In addition, parental involvement in the assessment process encourages consideration of culture and language factors and the role they may play in interpreting assessment results. Understanding the assessment challenges of students from culturally and linguistically diverse backgrounds is vital because this population of students is disproportionately represented in special education (see Abedi, 2006; Chu & Flores, 2011; Linn & Hemmer, 2011; U.S. Department of Education, 2016; Zhang & Katisyannis, 2002). Special education teachers must take an active role in communicating assessment data and gauging the understanding of all team members, paying particular attention to families' understandings.

Assessment results that are based on parental input encourage respectful treatment of families and values their expertise (Fish, 2008; Wolfe & Duran, 2013). Parents provide insights about their child, as well as discuss the goals they have for their child and what they hope the school can do to best support their child. Providing families with information about assessment data prior to eligibility and IEP meetings can help families prepare for team meetings, allowing them to generate questions they may have and alleviating feelings of being overwhelmed and having too much information to understand (Lo, 2008; Wolfe & Duran, 2013). The special education teacher may also serve as an advocate for the family. During meetings with the team, it is often the special education teacher's responsibility to make sure that assessment data are presented in clear and understandable terms and that all team members have time to ask questions and describe supports that they believe would be important for the student.

Providing families with information about assessment data prior to eligibility and IEP meetings can help families prepare for team meetings.

Finally, special education teachers are tasked with communicating initial and ongoing assessment data with other teachers and support staff. Students' IEPs are continually revised based on assessment data. Teachers and staff use assessment data to understand if interventions are effective and adjust instruction accordingly.

Policy and Research Support

According to federal regulations, IEP teams must include (a) parents; (b) at least one general education teacher; (c) at least one special education teacher; (d) a representative of the local education agency (typically an administrator); (e) someone who can interpret the instructional implications of evaluation results (can be one of the other listed members); (f) other individuals with expertise about the child; and, (g) when appropriate, the child (34 C.F.R. § 300.347[a][1]). The IDEA regulations also require that the IEP for a child with a disability include a statement of the child's current levels of educational performance (academic and behavioral). For an IEP team to accurately define this, the team must use relevant assessment data.

IDEA also stipulates that cultural and linguistic factors must be taken into consideration by the IEP team during assessment and interpretation of data (34 C.F.R. § 300.306[b][1]). Research has established that culturally and linguistically diverse students are frequently misidentified as having a disability (e.g., Rinaldi & Sampson, 2008; Samson & Lesaux, 2009). For example, it is often challenging to determine whether a student's difficulties are due to English acquisition or a learning disability, because students with these difficulties often display similar characteristics (Collier, 2011; Orosco & Klinger, 2010).

The assessment process must include the family's description of its resources, priorities, and concerns related to enhancing the child's development. This establishes assessment as family-directed and assists in ensuring that services take culture and language into account. After the appropriate administration of assessments, special education teachers review and communicate with other IEP team members the patterns of student strengths and needs and gain consensus from multiple stake-holders (e.g., parents, general education teachers, target students; Collier, 2011; Ortiz & Artiles, 2010). When necessary and appropriate, other professionals (e.g., English language learner teacher, bilingual evaluator) should join the IEP team to provide assistance with communicating and interpreting assessment results. In addition, special education teachers should encourage parental and, as appropriate, student collaboration. Families and the students themselves know their cultural and linguistic practices best and can educate the team regarding these practices (Barnard-Brak & Lechtenberger, 2009; Scott, Hauerwas, & Brown, 2014).

Research suggests that involving parents in the IEP process holds the potential for improving implementation and student outcomes. One way that parents demonstrate support of their children's education is by attending IEP meetings and volunteering. Children whose families are more involved show a variety of more positive outcomes than children with less family involvement, including (a) better grades, (b) more involvement in organized groups, and (c) more involvement in postschool employment (Newman, 2005; Test et al., 2009). Some evidence also indicates a positive association between students with disabilities participating in IEP meetings and their academic outcomes (Barnard-Brak & Lechtenberger, 2009).

Conclusion

Policy mandates the members of all IEP teams and factors that should be considered when assessing and interpreting the results of assessments of culturally and linguistically diverse students. However, the characteristics of each IEP team, along with the assessment data for each child, are unique. The special education teacher has a pivotal role in helping all members of the IEP team to understand assessment data. Such data provide the foundation for determining appropriate educational services for students with disabilities. Ongoing communication of assessment results assists with implementing effective IEPs and ensuring desirable outcomes for students with disabilities.

HLP6	Use student assessment data, analyze instructional practices, and make necessary adjustments that improve student outcomes.

After special education teachers develop instructional goals, they evaluate and make ongoing adjustments to students' instructional programs. Once instruction and other supports are designed and implemented, special education teachers have the skill to manage and engage in ongoing data collection using curriculum-based measures, informal classroom assessments, observations of student academic performance and behavior, self-assessment of classroom instruction, and discussions with key stakeholders (i.e., students, families, other professionals). Teachers study their practice to improve student learning, validate reasoned hypotheses about salient instructional features, and enhance instructional decision making. Effective teachers retain, reuse, and extend practices that improve student learning and adjust or discard those that do not.

Special education teachers identify effective instructional and behavioral practices to address the needs of individual students. Although these practices may be evidence-based or widely considered effective, the special education teacher recognizes that no single practice will be effective for every student. To determine the effect of instructional practices, special education teachers make instructional decisions based on data related to student progress toward well-defined goals. This type of formative assessment is "a process used by teachers and students during instruction that provides feedback to adjust ongoing teaching and learning to improve students' achievement of intended instructional outcomes" (McManus, 2008, p. 3).

Formative assessment requires collecting data from a range of sources (e.g., curriculum-based measures, informal class-room assessments, observation of classroom performance, self-assessment of classroom instruction; Popham, 2008)—and using these data to inform a cycle of continuous improvement (What Works Clearinghouse [WWC], 2009b). This cycle includes (a) collecting a variety of data regarding student learning from valid sources, (b) interpreting the data to determine the effectiveness of instruction, (c) developing alternative instructional approaches as necessary, (d) modifying instruction, and (f) continuing the cycle by collecting additional data to determine the effectiveness of the instructional change. To improve student achievement, formative assessment data may be used to make instructional changes such as:

- prioritizing the use of instructional time to increase student opportunities to learn,

> *Formative assessment ... is only effective when coupled with sound instructional decision making and effective interventions.*

- providing additional instruction for students who are struggling to learn particular content,
- modifying delivery strategies,
- refining instruction, and
- determining if the curriculum needs to be adapted based on student strengths and weaknesses after examining grade level or schoolwide data (WWC, 2009b).

Research and Policy Support

The accountability for student achievement that was mandated in the No Child Left Behind Act of 2001 (now Every Student Succeeds Act) resulted in increased attention to assessment for instructional decision making on the part of teachers, school administrators, policy makers, and researchers. These professionals thus anticipated that "results from formative assessments could provide timely and descriptive information about students to help teachers plan for and deliver effective individualized instruction" (Gallagher & Worth, 2008, p. 1). Although there is no national policy mandate related to formative assessment, several states have policies or provide program guidance related to the use of formative assessment to improve instructional outcomes (Gallagher & Worth, 2008). Further, the U.S. Department of Education encourages local schools to use data for continuous improvement (Mandinach & Gummer, 2013), and formative assessment was one of the four pillars of the Race to the Top initiative (U.S. Department of Education, 2009).

Research evidence to support the use of formative assessment or a cycle of instructional improvement has been provided primarily by qualitative and descriptive studies, and is characterized as "low" by the Institute of Education Sciences (WWC, 2009b). However, researchers (e.g., Mandinach & Gummer, 2013) have supported the use of formative assessment as a logical and pragmatic approach to continuous improvement that leads to more effective instructional practices. A primary difficulty that arises when addressing the effectiveness of formative assessment relates to the fact that this process is not an instructional intervention, and is only effective when coupled with sound instructional decision making and effective interventions that are derived from a cycle of instructional improvement. Formative data can be used to guide instructional decision making toward more effective instructional strategies for students who are struggling with academic content. Examples of effective instructional strategies include direct instruction, strategy instruction, student feedback, reciprocal teaching, and peer tutoring (Hattie, 2008).

Researchers have noted that a critical issue with formative assessment is the appropriate use of data to guide instructional decisions (Coburn & Turner, 2012; Waldron, Parker, & McLeskey, 2014; WWC, 2009b). Although there is a dearth of research on the use of schoolwide data systems that are used for all grade levels and academic areas, research has been conducted on the use of data to guide instruction for students with disabilities and others who struggle to learn in elementary schools as part of multitiered systems of support (MTSS; L. Fuchs & Vaughn, 2012; Lembke & Stecker, 2007; Shapiro, Zigmond, Wallace, & Marston, 2011; Stecker et al., 2005; WWC, 2009a). Research has shown that such data systems are often part of schools that are effective and inclusive (Hehir & Katzmann, 2012; McLeskey, Waldron, & Redd, 2014).

A WWC report (2009b) noted that teachers are often asked to use student data without guidance regarding how this should be done. To address this need, school administrators should:

- provide a school-based facilitator who meets with teachers and teacher teams to discuss the systematic use of data for instructional decision making and provides professional development (including coaching) for teachers,

- provide structured time for teachers to collaborate related to data use and instructional decision making, and

- ensure that targeted professional development is regularly provided based on teacher needs to improve data literacy and data use. (WWC, 2009b)

These recommendations have been supported and extended by those involved in using data as part of MTSS (e.g., Stecker et al., 2005; WWC, 2009a). For example, decision-making rules should be used for interpreting curriculum-based measurement data to support teachers in making instructional decisions. In addition, research related to MTSS has revealed that teachers benefit from instructional consultation from knowledgeable consultants or computerized systems to improve the quantity and quality of instructional changes that lead to improved student outcomes.

Conclusion

Although research support for the use of formative assessment or a cycle of continuous improvement of instruction has been characterized as "low" by the Institute of Education Sciences, many individual studies support the use of assessment data as part of a data-based decision making framework to improve instruction. This is especially the case when teachers are working with students with unique educational needs.

References

Abedi, J. (2006). Psychometric issues in the ELL assessment and special education eligibility. *Teachers College Record, 108*, 2282-2303. doi:10.1111/j.1467-9620.2006.00782.x

Al Otaiba, S., & Fuchs, D. (2006). Who are the young children for whom best practices in reading are ineffective? An experimental and longitudinal study. *Journal of Learning Disabilities, 39*, 414-431. doi:10.1177/00222194060390050401

Barnard-Brak, L.., & Lechtenberger, D. (2009). Student IEP participation and academic achievement across time. *Remedial and Special Education, 31*, 343-349. doi:10.1177/0741932509338382

Bishop, A. G., Brownell, M. T., Klingner, J. K., Leko, M. M., & Galman, S. A. C. (2010). Differences in beginning special education teachers: the influence of personal attributes, preparation, and school environment on classroom reading practices. *Learning Disability Quarterly, 33*, 75-92

Brownell, M. T., Dimino, J., Bishop, A. G., Haager, D., Gersten, R., Menon, S., ... Penfield, R. D. (2009). The role of domain expertise in beginning special education teacher quality. *Exceptional Children, 75*, 391-411

Brownell, M. T., Haager, D., Bishop, A. G., Klingner, J. K., Menon, S., Penfield, R., & Dingle, M. (2007, April). *Teacher quality in special education: The role of knowledge, classroom practice, and school environment*. Paper presented at the annual meeting of the American Education Research Association, Chicago.

Brownell, M. T., Lauterbach, A. A., Dingle, M. P., Boardman, A. G., Urbach, J. E., Leko, M., ... Park, Y. (2014). Individual and contextual factors influencing special education teacher learning in Literacy Learning Cohorts. *Learning Disabilities Quarterly, 34*, 31-44. doi:10.1177/0731948713487179

Caffrey, E., Fuchs, D., & Fuchs, L. S. (2008). The predictive validity of dynamic assessment: A review. *The Journal of Special Education, 41*, 254-270. doiL10.1177/0022466907310366

Caffrey, Fuchs, & Fuchs, 2008; Fuchs et al., 2008

Chu, S., & Flores, S. (2011). Assessment of English language learners with learning disabilities. *Clearing House, 84*, 244-248. doi:10.1080/00098655.2011.590550

Center for Parent Information and Resources (2014, May). *Evaluating children for disability*. Retrieved from http://www.parentcenterhub.org/repository/evaluation/

Coburn, C. & Turner, E. (2012). The practice of data use: An introduction. *American Journal of Education, 118*, 99–111. doi:10.1086/663272

Collier, V. (2011). *Seven steps to separating difference from disability*. Thousand Oaks, CA: Corwin Press.

Council for Exceptional Children. (n.d.). *Individualized education programs*. Retrieved from https://www.cec.sped.org/Special-Ed-Topics/Specialty-Areas/Individualized-Education-Programs

Deno, S. L., Fuchs, L. S., Marston, D. B., & Shin, J. (2001). Using curriculum-based measurement to develop growth standards for students with learning disabilities. *School Psychology Review, 30*, 507-524.

Fish, W. W. (2008). The IEP meeting: Perceptions of parents of students who receive special education services. *Preventing School Failure: Alternative Education for Children and Youth, 53*, 8–14. doi:10.3200/PSFL.53.1.8-14

Fletcher, J. M., Stuebing, K. K., Barth, A. E., Denton, C. A., Cirino, P. T., Francis, D. J., & Vaughn, S. (2011). Cognitive correlates of inadequate response to reading intervention. *School Psychology Review, 40*, 3–22.

Fuchs, D., Compton, D. L., Fuchs, L. S., Bryant, V. J., Hamlett, C. L., & Lambert, W. (2012). First-grade cognitive abilities as long term predictors of reading comprehension and disability status. *Journal of Learning Disabilities, 45*, 217–231. doi: 10.1177/0022219412442154

Fuchs, L., & Vaughn, S. (2012). Responsiveness-to-intervention: A decade later. *Journal of Learning Disabilities, 45*, 195–203. doi:10.1177/0022219412442150

Gallagher, C. & Worth, P. (2008). *Formative assessment policies, programs, and practices in the Southwest Region* (Issues & Answers Report, REL 2008–No. 041). Washington, DC: U.S. Department of Education, Institute of Education Sciences.

Hammer, C. S., Komaroff, E., Rodriquez, B. L., Lopez, L. M., Scarpino, S. E., & Goldstein, B. (2012). Predicting Spanish–English bilingual children's language abilities. *Journal of Speech, Language, and Hearing Research, 55*, 1251-1264. doi:10.1044/1092-4388(2012/11-0016)

Hammond, H., Ingalls, L., & Trussell, R. P. (2008). Family members' involvement in the initial individual education program (IEP) meeting and the IEP process: Perceptions and reactions. *International Journal about Parents in Education, 2*, 35–48.

Hattie, J. (2008). *Visible learning: A synthesis of over 800 meta-analyses relating to achievement*. New York, NY: Routledge.

Hehir, T., & Katzman, L. (2012). *Effective inclusive schools: Designing successful schoolwide programs*. San Francisco, CA: Jossey-Bass

IDEA regulations, 34 C.F.R. § 300 (2012).

Individuals With Disabilities Education Act, 20 U.S.C. §§ 1400 *et seq*. (2006 & Supp. V. 2011)

Judge, S., & Bell, S. M. (2010). Reading achievement trajectories for students with learning disabilities during the elementary school years. *Reading and Writing Quarterly: Overcoming Learning Difficulties, 27*, 153-178. doi:10.1080/10573 569.2011.532722

Katz, L. A., Stone, C. A., Carlisle, J. F., Corey, D. L., & Zeng, J. (2008). Initial progress of children identified with disabilities in Michigan's Reading First schools. *Exceptional Children, 74*, 235-256. doi:10.1177/001440290807400206

Lembke, E. & Stecker, P. (2007). *Curriculum-based measurement in mathematics*. Portsmouth, NH: RCM Research Corporation, Center on Instruction.

Leslie, L., & Caldwell, J. S. (2015). *Qualitative reading inventory* (5th ed.). New York, NY: Pearson.

Linn, D., & Hemmer, L. (2011). English language learner disproportionality in special education: Implications for the scholar-practitioner. *Journal of Educational Research and Practice, 1*, 70-80. doi:10.5590/JERAP.2011.01.1.06

Lo, L. (2008). Chinese families' level of participation and experiences in IEP meetings. *Preventing School Failure: Alternative Education for Children and Youth, 53*, 21-27. doi:10.3200/PSFL.53.1.21-27

Mandinach, E. B., & Gummer, E. S. (2013). Defining data literacy: A report on a convening of experts. *Journal of Educational Research and Policy Studies, 13*, 6-28.

McLeskey, J., Waldron, N., & Redd, L. (2014). A case study of a highly effective, inclusive elementary school. *The Journal of Special Education, 48*, 59-70. doi:10.1177/0022466912440455

McManus, S. (2008). *Attributes of effective formative assessment*. Washington, DC: Council of Chief State School Officers.

Montague, M. (1996). Assessing mathematical problem solving. *Learning Disabilities Research and Practice, 11*, 238-248.

Murray C,, & Greenberg, M. T. (2006). Examining the importance of social relationships and social contexts in the lives of children with high-incidence disabilities. *The Journal of Special Education, 39*, 220-233. doi:10.1177/00224 669060390040301

The National Dissemination Center for Children with Disabilities. (n.d.). *What is a multidisciplinary evaluation and assessment?* Retrieved from http://www.mychildwithoutlimits.org/plan/early-intervention/multidisciplinary-evaluation-and-assessment/

Newman, L. (2005, March). *Family involvement in the educational development of youth with disabilities. A special topic report of findings from the National Longitudinal Transition Study-2* (NLTS2). Menlo Park, CA: SRI International. Retrieved from http://www.nlts2.org/reports/2005_03/nlts2_report_2005_03_complete.pdf

Orosco, M., & Klingner, J. (2010). One school's implementation of RTI with English language learners: Referring into RTI. *Journal of Learning Disabilities, 43*, 269–288. doi:10.1177/0022219409355474

Ortiz, A. A., & Artiles, A. J. (2010). Meeting the needs of ELLs with disabilities: A linguistically and culturally responsive model. In G. Li & P. A. Edwards (Eds.), *Best practices in ELL instruction* (pp. 247–272). New York, NY: Guilford.

Popham, J. (2008). *Transformative assessment*. Alexandria, VA: ASCD.

Rinaldi, C., & Samson, J. (2008). English language learners and response to intervention: Referral considerations. *TEACHING Exceptional Children, 40*(5), 6–14. doi:10.1177/004005990804000501

Samson, J. F., & Lesaux, N. K. (2009). Language-minority learners in special education: Rates and predictors of identification for services. *Journal of Learning Disabilities, 42*, 148–162. doi:10.1177/0022219408326221

Scott, A. N., Haurwas, L. B., & Brown, R. D. (2014). State policy and guidance for identifying learning disabilities in culturally and linguistically diverse students. *Learning Disability Quarterly, 37*, 172–185. doi:10.1177/0731948713507261

Seo, S. (2006). *Special education reading teachers' understandings and enactment of motivational teaching for elementary students with learning disabilities* (Doctoral dissertation). ProQuest Dissertations and Theses database. (UMI No. 3228836)

Seo, S., Brownell, M. T., Bishop, A. G., & Dingle, M. (2008). Beginning special education teachers' classroom reading instruction: Practices that engage elementary students with learning disabilities. *Exceptional Children, 75*, 97–122.

Shapiro, E., Zigmond, N., Wallace, T., & Marston, D. (Eds.) (2011). *Models for implementing response to intervention: Tools, outcomes, and implications.* New York, NY: Guilford.

Stecker, P. M., Fuchs, L. S., & Fuchs, D. (2005). Using curriculum–based measurement to improve student achievement: Review of research. *Psychology in the Schools, 42*, 795–819.

Test, D. W., Mazzotti, V. L., Mustain, A. L., Fowler, C. H., Kortering, L., & Kohler, P. (2009). Evidence-based secondary transition predictors for improving postschool outcomes for students with disabilities. *Career Development for Exceptional Individuals, 32*, 160–181. doi:10.1177/0885728809346960

U.S. Department of Education (2009). *Race to the Top program: Executive summary*. Washington, DC: Author. Retrieved from https://www2.ed.gov/programs/racetothetop/executive-summary.pdf

U.S. Department of Education (2016). *Racial and ethnic disparities in special education*. Washington, DC: Office of Special Education and Rehabilitation. Retrieved from http://www2.ed.gov/programs/osepidea/618-data/LEA-racial-ethnic-disparities-tables/disproportionality-analysis-by-state-analysis-category.pdf

Vaughn, S., & Bos, C. (2014). *Strategies for teaching students with learning and behavior problems* (9th ed.). Boston, MA: Allyn & Bacon.

Vaughn, S., Linan-Thompson, S., & Hickman, P. (2003). Response to intervention as a means of identifying students with reading/learning disabilities. *Exceptional Children, 69*, 391–400. doi:10.1177/001440290306900401

Waldron, N., Parker, J., & McLeskey, J. (2014). How are data systems used in inclusive schools? In J. McLeskey, N. Waldron, F. Spooner, & B. Algozzine (Eds.), *Handbook of effective inclusive schools: Research and practice* (pp. 155–166). New York, NY: Routledge.

What Works Clearinghouse. (2009a, February). Assisting students struggling with reading: response to intervention and multi-tier intervention in the primary grades (NCEE 2009-4045). Washington, DC: U.S. Department of Education, Institute of Education Sciences. Retrieved from https://ies.ed.gov/ncee/wwc/Docs/PracticeGuide/rti_reading_pg_021809.pdf

What Works Clearinghouse. (2009b, September). *Using student achievement data to support instructional decision making* (NCEE 2009-4067). Washington, DC: U.S. Department of Education, Institute of Education Sciences. Retrieved from http://ies.ed.gov/ncee/wwc/Docs/PracticeGuide/dddm_pg_092909.pdf

Wolfe, K., & Duran, L. K. (2013). Culturally and linguistically diverse parents' perceptions of the IEP process: A review of current research. *Multiple Voices for Ethnically Diverse Exceptional Learners, 13*(2), 4–18.

Zhang, D., & Katsiyannis, A. (2002). Minority representation in special education: A persistent challenge. *Remedial & Special Education, 23*, 180–187. doi:10.1177/07419325020230030601

Research Syntheses: Social/Emotional/Behavioral High-Leverage Practices

Effective special education teachers establish a consistent, organized, and respectful learning environment to support student success. To do this, they employ several practices that are critical in promoting student social and emotional well-being. First, effective teachers focus on increasing appropriate behavior by adopting an instructional approach that incorporates the explicit teaching of social skills and offers students multiple opportunities to practice appropriate social behaviors throughout the school day followed by positive specific feedback. Second, they implement evidence-based practices to prevent social, emotional, and behavioral challenges and provide early intervention at the first sign of risk. Third, effective teachers provide increasingly comprehensive supports through a team-based problem-solving strategy, to match the intensity of student challenges guided by behavioral assessment. Finally, they implement all behavioral supports—even those in response to significant problem behavior—in a caring, respectful, and culturally relevant manner. Effective teachers recognize that academic and behavioral support strategies are more effective when delivered within the context of positive and caring teacher-student relationships.

HLP7	**Establish a consistent, organized, and respectful learning environment.**

To build and foster positive relationships, teachers should establish age-appropriate and culturally responsive expectations, routines, and procedures within their classrooms that are positively stated and explicitly taught and practiced across the school year. When students demonstrate mastery and follow established rules and routines, teachers should provide age-appropriate specific performance feedback in meaningful and caring ways. By establishing, following, and reinforcing expectations of all students within the classroom, teachers will reduce the potential for challenging behavior and increase student engagement. When establishing learning environments, teachers should build mutually respectful relationships with students and engage them in setting the classroom climate (e.g., rules and routines); be respectful; and value ethnic, cultural, contextual, and linguistic diversity to foster student engagement across learning environments.

Special educators cannot "make" students learn or behave; they can, however, create environments to increase the likelihood that students do both (Lewis, 2009). The foundation of any effective learning environment includes clear and consistent rules, routines, and procedures that keep students engaged and on track throughout the school day. All classroom procedures should be implemented in a proactive and positive manner in which the special educator is always the exemplar in treating students and other adults in a respectful and caring manner.

Rules should be stated positively (i.e., what the teacher wants students to do rather than does not want them to do) and kept to five or fewer. Examples and non-examples of behavioral expectations should be directly taught and expectations should be practiced throughout the school year until students demonstrate mastery.

Routines such as entering and exiting the classroom, how to respond to the teacher's attention signal, how to seek assistance, and expectations during activity transitions should be considered, as well as other daily routines. Critical steps to comply with procedures and routines should be task-analyzed and explicitly taught and practiced with students.

The conventional recommended ratio found in the professional literature is for every corrective statement a teacher makes, educators should look for at least four opportunities to acknowledge appropriate behavior (i.e., student demonstrations of classroom expectations). The goal is to acknowledge student mastery of social-behavioral expectations and compliance with procedures, not to point out frequent errors.

Special educators should provide students with opportunities to respond to both social and academic requests throughout the day, and prompts should reflect the nature of the academic or social expectation (e.g., "who can tell me what voice level we use when we walk to lunch?"). The rate of opportunities to respond will vary across age and severity of disability, but should be a primary instructional strategy during acquisition and fluency building among all students.

Special educators should strive for a balance of direct instruction, multiple opportunities for students to practice with high rates of feedback, and high rates of student success (i.e., 80% or better proficiency on tasks) to promote high engagement time and low rates of off-task behavior. For every lesson, student learning progress should be carefully monitored and instruction, practice, and feedback adjusted accordingly.

Research Support

A clear body of evidence exists to support these classroom strategies, as well as several others (see Hattie, 2008, for a comprehensive review). Researchers have examined combinations of the above on both academic and social behavior effects (Armendariz & Umbreit, 1999; Blackwell & McLaughlin, 2005; Bowman-Perrott. 2009; Haydon et al., 2010; Lewis, Hudson, Richter, & Johnson, 2004; Spencer, Scruggs, & Mastropieri, 2003; Sutherland, Wehby, & Yoder, 2002) and the essential features to increase teacher use of evidence-based practices (Simonsen, Fairbanks, Briesch, Myers, & Sugai, 2008; Simonsen, Myers, & DeLuca, 2010; Stichter et al., 2009; Wehby, Tally, & Falk, 2004). The Institute for Education Science's What Works Clearinghouse has indicated these and several similar strategies as having moderate to strong empirical evidence at the elementary level (What Works Clearinghouse, 2008).

Conclusion

Establishing a clear, consistent, and positive learning environment serves as the foundation for all other high-leverage practices (HLPs). It increases the likelihood of student academic and social behavior success, it increases educator opportunities to engage in effective instructional practices, and it fosters caring and respectful interactions between educators and students. Research over the past 50 years consistently reaffirms the effects that classroom management and instruction have on both academic and social performance (Hattie, 2008).

HLP8	Provide positive and constructive feedback to guide students' learning and behavior.

The purpose of feedback is to guide student learning and behavior and increase student motivation, engagement, and independence, leading to improved student learning and behavior. Effective feedback must be strategically delivered and goal directed; feedback is most effective when the learner has a goal and the feedback informs the learner regarding areas needing improvement and ways to improve performance. Feedback may be verbal, nonverbal, or written, and should be timely, contingent, genuine, meaningful, age appropriate, and at rates commensurate with task and phase of learning (i.e., acquisition, fluency, maintenance). Teachers should provide ongoing feedback until learners reach their established learning goals.

Note. As discussed in the Preface, two research syntheses were developed for the practice of providing effective feedback; this item appears in both the Social/Emotional/Behavioral Practices HLPs and the Instruction HLPs.

There is a common misconception that high rates of positive reinforcement will do "harm" to students' intrinsic motivation or "don't work." *Positive reinforcement* means that when the environment contingently follows a student's behavior with an action, and that behavior maintains or increases, whatever followed the behavior is reinforcing to the student. Just like academic skill mastery, if teachers want students to build social behavior skill mastery they must provide specific, contingent feedback. If students make social behavior learning errors, (i.e., problem behavior), feedback should focus on what social skill the student should have used (Lewis, Jones, Horner, & Sugai, 2010). If students demonstrate the appropriate social skill, feedback should acknowledge student effort and include the classroom expectation or rule (e.g, "I see you are working hard to be a 'respectful' learner: You are working quietly so others can learn").

> *Just like academic skill mastery, if teachers want students to build social behavior skill mastery they must provide specific, contingent feedback.*

The idea that students should always be motivated intrinsically simply is not possible. Activities that are *intrinsically motivating* are those that in and of themselves are reinforcing to the individual (Ryan & Deci, 2000). Unfortunately, most students do not find writing reports or solving algebra problems intrinsically motivating. What special educators should do is use actions and activities that are extrinsically motivating, but work toward student self-regulation of those motivators. For example, the goal is for students to complete a difficult math assignment not because the assignment is intrinsically motivating (i.e., inherently fun and enjoyable) but rather because they choose to engage in the task (i.e., self-regulation) because they know it will lead to an outcome that is reinforcing (i.e., free

time, acknowledgment from parents—both of which are extrinsic motivators; Ryan & Deci, 2000).

Research Support

From early seminal work such as the "good behavior game" (Medland & Stachnik, 1972) and Brophy's (1981) work on key teacher behaviors within effective classrooms, there is a strong literature base to support the use of positive specific feedback to acknowledge and increase academic and social skill mastery (Alberto & Troutman, 2013; Darch & Kame'enui, 2004; Lewis et al., 2010; Nelson & Roberts, 2000; Simonsen & Myers, 2105; Stichter & Lewis, 2006; Sutherland, Alder, & Gunter, 2003; Sutherland, Wehby, & Copeland, 2000; Sutherland et al,, 2002). The theoretical work to disprove the impact of acknowledgment is limited and often misinterprets conceptual frameworks or demonstrates limitations of external motivators within constrained research methodology (Ryan & Deci, 2000).

Conclusion

Confusion over terms such as *intrinsic* and *extrinsic* motivation, *reinforcement*, *rewards*, *praise*, and similar terms continues—often intentionally by authors wishing to push their theoretical view, and many times inadvertently by well-meaning educators. If educators want to teach skills to mastery and have them maintained and generalized beyond the school day, specific positive feedback, as well as corrective instructional feedback when learning errors occur, is an essential and crucial element of the teaching and learning process. This simple yet highly effective element of learning environments promotes both academic and social success.

HLP9	Teach social behaviors.

Teachers should explicitly teach appropriate interpersonal skills, including communication, and self-management, aligning lessons with classroom and schoolwide expectations for student behavior. Prior to teaching, teachers should determine the nature of the social skill challenge. If students do not know how to perform a targeted social skill, direct social skill instruction should be provided until mastery is achieved. If students display performance problems, the appropriate social skill should initially be taught, then emphasis should shift to prompting the student to use the skill and ensuring the "appropriate" behavior accesses the same or a similar outcome (i.e., is reinforcing to the student) as the problem behavior.

An often noted concern regarding students with disabilities is their struggles to interact socially with adults and peers in appropriate ways. Regardless of disability category or overall emphasis of the student's individualized education program, for most students special educators should include social skill instruction as part of their daily curriculum. Similar to academic skills, social skills should be taught through direct instruction, students should be given multiple opportunities to practice targeted skills, and positive specific feedback should be given when targeted social skills are displayed (Sugai & Lewis, 1996). There are specific, empirically validated components of effective social skill instruction, including assessing and identifying students' social skill patterns, using a "tell-show-practice" instructional format, and assessing students' skill mastery and generalization across time and settings.

Although there are several quality social skill curriculums widely available, most approach social skills as if the student has a skill "deficit"; that is, the student does not know how to display the appropriate social skill. For students with moderate to severe disabilities, including autism spectrum disorder and intellectual disability, this might be the case. For most students with mild

disabilities, however, social skill challenges are often "performance" problems. In other words, the student knows what social skill they should use under specific conditions (e.g., "count to 10 when I get angry") but displays an inappropriate skill because it leads to outcomes that maintain the problem skill (e.g., "if I throw things, I am removed from the classroom and I am no longer angry"). It is essential to match the focus and outcome of each social skill lesson to the student problem type (i.e., deficit or performance).

Within each lesson, the special educator should first identify and define the social skill and when to use it (e.g., "When you are angry, the first thing you do is stop"). Second, after discussing what it means to be angry and a range of ways to "stop," (tell), the teacher should demonstrate (show) a range of appropriate ways to stop and also inappropriate ways to stop (i.e., the non-example or social skills the student is currently using that have been labeled inappropriate). Following examples and non-examples, the student should practice using only the appropriate social skill through role plays.

Teaching social skills within a small group format is generally straightforward and successful; the challenge is promoting generalization and maintenance of learned skills. Strategies such as teaching directly within targeted settings, providing frequent prompts or reminders to use newly learned skills, and providing high rates of positive specific feedback are all empirically validated strategies to promote generalized responding over time.

Research Support

With hundreds of social skill instruction investigations conducted to date, the evidence of effectiveness for these strategies has long been established (Ang & Hughes, 2001; Beelman, Pfingsten, & Losel, 1994; Cook et al., 2008; Losel & Beelman, 2003; Gresham, 2002b; Mikami, Jia, & Na, 2014). As with all interventions as broad and encompassing as "social skill instruction," contra-indicated findings on effectiveness also exist (e.g., Quinn, Kavale, Mathur, Rutherford, & Forness, 1999). However, when intervention is matched to a presenting problem, sufficient treatment dosage is in effect, and contextual factors are programmed into instruction to promote generalized findings, social skill instruction continues to demonstrate improved social functioning among students with disabilities (Gresham, 2002a; Gresham, Sugai, & Horner, 2001).

Conclusion

The ability to interact with adults and peers and to manage one's own behavior across settings is essential to student success. Unfortunately, students with disabilities often do not master these essential social skills in ways typically developing children do and therefore these must be explicitly taught. Social skill instruction has been found to improve social functional from preschool through adulthood, across a variety of social skill challenges, and among a range of disabilities. The balance of the empirical evidence indicates that social skill instruction, paired with generalization strategies, can lead to improved social-emotional functioning of students with disabilities.

HLP10	Conduct functional behavioral assessments to develop individual student behavior support plans.

Creating individual behavior plans is a central role of all special educators. Key to successful plans is to conduct a functional behavioral assessment (FBA) any time behavior is chronic, intense, or impedes learning. A comprehensive FBA results in a hypothesis about the function of the student's problem behavior. Once the function is determined, a behavior intervention plan is developed that (a) teaches the student a pro-social replacement behavior that will serve the same or similar function, (b) alters the environment to make the replacement behavior more efficient and effective than the problem behavior, (c) alters the environment to no longer allow the problem behavior to access the previous outcome, and (d) includes ongoing data collection to monitor progress.

Functional behavioral assessments (FBA) are routinely conducted—and in some instances required by Individuals With Disabilities Education Act (IDEA; 2006) regulations—to determine what occasions and what maintains current patterns of student problem behavior. Using indirect methods such as rating scales, interviews, and archival data search (e.g., student file, discipline and attendance reports) and direct methods that involve a trained observer watching during problematic periods, hypotheses regarding the possible function of the problem behavior are developed using the following format (Lewis, Mitchell, Harvey, Green, & McKenzie, 2015):

- When [*conditions that trigger problem behavior, such as a worksheet that requires extensive writing*],

- The student will [*target problem behavior*],

- To get or avoid [*the outcome that maintains the behavior, such as getting peer attention or avoiding difficult tasks*].

Once a hypothesis is developed, a behavior support plan to address the function of the problem behavior is developed which includes a plan to teach a pro-social replacement behavior that results in the same or similar outcome (e.g., get attention or avoid a difficult task; Scott & Kamps, 2007). The plan should also include classroom and other learning environmental modifications that ensure (a) that when the student demonstrates the replacement behavior, the same or similar outcomes occur at high rates (e.g., student raises hand, teacher immediately recognizes and reinforces the student to give high rates of attention); and (b) that if the student demonstrates the problem behavior, the hypothesized function of the behavior is not accessed (e.g., student calls out instead of raising hand, teacher ignores and attends to a peer who did raise hand; Scott & Kamps, 2007).

Research and Policy Support

Given the highly individualized nature of the FBA–behavior support plan process, the majority of research conducted to date has employed the use of single-subject designs. Since the early 1980s, FBA research has moved from clinical settings targeting young adults with severe cognitive impairments (Carr & Durand, 1985; Iwata, Dorsey, Slifer, Bauman, & Richman, 1982) to a variety of school, home, and community settings focusing on students with mild disabilities (Lalli, Browder, Mace & Brown, 1993; Northup et al., 1981) as well as students at risk for disabilities (Kamps et al., 1995; Kern, Childs, Dunlap, Clarke & Falk, 1994; Lewis & Sugai, 1996a, 1996b; Umbreit, 1995). Since 1997, IDEA regulations have required FBAs be conducted if students with disabilities are removed from school due to disciplinary infractions 10 days or more (34 C.F.R. § 300.530), and a wide range of studies have been conducted across multiple groups of research teams (e.g., Gage, Lewis, & Stichter, 2012; Solnick & Ardoin, 2010; Wood, Blair, & Ferro, 2009). FBA-based interventions have been found to be more efficient and effective in reducing challenging behavior among students with disabilities and those at high risk than non-function-based interventions (Gage et al., 2012; Ingram, Lewis-Palmer, & Sugai, 2005; Liaupsin, Umbreit, Ferro, Urso, & Upreti, 2006; Newcomer & Lewis, 2004; Park & Scott, 2009; Payne, Scott, & Conroy, 2007; Stichter, Lewis, Johnson, & Trussell, 2004).

Conclusion

FBA-based intervention planning has a wide range of empirical work to support its use as an effective practice in addressing intensive challenging behavior. There is no clearly delineated set of practices that make up a comprehensive FBA, but the elements listed above are routinely cited in the relevant research. Although the nature of conducting FBA-based intervention research does not lend itself to the current What Works Clearinghouse requirement for multiple randomized control trials, both the Institute of Education Sciences and the Council for Exceptional Children have created guidelines for the inclusion of single-subject research to be considered in establishing evidence-based practices. Based on the studies cited here, as well as numerous others, the practice may be considered as meeting the minimal standards for being evidence-based.

References

Alberto, P. A., & Troutman, A. C. (2013). *Applied behavior analysis for teachers* (9th ed.). Upper Saddle River, NJ: Pearson Education.

Ang, R., & Hughes, J. (2001). Differential benefits of skills training with antisocial youth base on group composition: A meta-analytic investigation. *School Psychology Review, 31*, 164–185.

Armendariz, F. & Umbreit, J. (1999). Using active responding to reduce disruptive behavior in a general education classroom. *Journal of Positive Behavior Interventions, 1*, 152–158. doi:10.1177/109830079900100303

Beelman, A., Pfingsten, U., & Losel, F. (1994). Effects of training social competence in children: A meta-analysis of recent evaluation studies. *Journal of Clinical Child Psychology, 23*, 260–271. doi:10.1207/s15374424jccp2303_4

Blackwell, A. J. & McLaughlin, T. F. (2005). Using guided notes, choral responding, and response cards to increase student performance. *The International Journal of Special Education, 20*, 1–5.

Bowman-Perrott, L. (2009). Class-wide peer tutoring: An effective strategy for students with emotional and behavioral disorders. *Intervention in School and Clinic, 44*, 259–267. doi:10.1177/1053451208330898

Brophy, J. H. (1981). Teacher praise: A functional analysis. *Review of Educational Research, 51*, 5–32. doi:10.3102/00346543051001005

Carr, E. G., & Durand, M. V. (1985). Reducing behavior problems through functional communication training. *Journal of Applied Behavior Analysis, 18*, 111–126. doi:10.1901/jaba.1985.18-111

Cook, C. R., Gresham, F. M., Kern, L. Barreras, R. B., Thornton, S, & Crews, S. D. (2008). Social skills training for secondary students with emotional and/or behavioral disorders: A review and analysis of the meta-analytic literature. *Journal of Emotional and Behavioral Disorders, 16*, 131–144. doi:10.1177/1063426608314541

Darch, C. B., & Kame'enui, E. B. (2004). *Instructional classroom management: A proactive approach to behavior management* (2nd ed.). Upper Saddle River, NJ: Pearson Education.

Gage, N. A., Lewis, T. J., & Stichter, J. P. (2012). Functional behavioral assessment-based interventions for students with or at-risk for emotional and/or behavioral disorders in school: A hierarchical linear modeling meta-analysis. *Behavioral Disorders, 37*, 55–77.

Gresham, F. M. (2002a). Best practices in social skills training. In A. Thomas & J. Grimes (Eds.), *Best practices in school psychology IV* (pp. 1029-1040). Washington, DC: National Association of School Psychologists.

Gresham, F. M. (2002b). Teaching social skills to high-risk children and youth: Preventive and remedial strategies. In M. R. Shinn, H. M. Walker, & G. Stoner (Eds.), *Interventions for academic behavior problems II: Preventive and remedial approaches* (pp. 403-432). Washington, DC: National Association of School Psychologists.

Gresham, F. M., Sugai, G. & Horner, R. H. (2001). Interpreting outcomes of social skills training for students with high-incidence disabilities. *Exceptional Children, 67*, 331-344.

Hattie, J. A. C. (2008). *Visible learning: A synthesis of over 800 meta-analyses relating to achievement.* New York, NY: Routledge.

Haydon, T., Conroy, M. A., Scott, T. M., Sindelar, P. T., Barber, B. R., & Orlando, A. (2010). A comparison of three types of opportunities to respond on student academic and social behaviors. *Journal of Emotional and Behavioral Disorders, 18*, 27-40. doi:10.1177/1063426609333448

Ingram, K., Lewis-Palmer, T., & Sugai, G. (2005). Function-based intervention planning: Comparing the effectiveness of FBA indicated and contra-indicated intervention plans. *Journal of Positive Behavior Interventions, 7,* 224-236. doi:10.1177/10983007050070040401

Iwata, B. A., Dorsey, M. F., Slifer, K. J., Bauman, K. E., & Richman, G. S. (1982). Toward a functional analysis of self injury. *Analysis and Intervention in Developmental Disabilities, 2*, 3-20. doi:10.1016/0270-4684(82)90003-9

Kamps, D. M., Ellis, C., Mancina, C., Wyble, J., Greene, L., & Harvey, D. (1995). Case studies using functional analysis for young children with behavior risks. *Education and Treatment of Children, 18*, 243-260.

Kern, L., Childs, K. E., Dunlap, G., Clarke, S., & Falk, G. D. (1994). Using assessment-based curricular intervention to improve the classroom behavior of a student with emotional and behavioral challenges. *Journal of Applied Behavior Analysis, 27*, 7-19. doi:10.1901/jaba.1994.27-7

Lalli, J. S., Browder, D. M., Mace, F. C., & Brown, D. K. (1993). Teacher use of descriptive analysis data to implement interventions to decrease students' problem behaviors. *Journal of Applied Behavior Analysis, 26,* 227-238. doi:10.1901/jaba.1993.26-227

Lewis, T. J. (2009, June). *Are we there yet? Mapping the PBS course for the long haul.* Keynote presentation at the 4th Annual Missouri Schoolwide Positive Behavior Support Summer Institute, Osage Beach, MO.

Lewis, T. J., Hudson, S., Richter, M., & Johnson, N. (2004). Scientifically supported practices in EBD: A proposed approach and brief review of current practices. *Behavioral Disorders, 29*, 247–259.

Lewis, T. J., Jones, S. E. L., Horner, R. H., & Sugai, G. (2010). School-wide positive behavior support and students with emotional/behavioral disorders: implications for prevention, identification and intervention. *Exceptionality 18*(2), 82–93. doi:10.1080/09362831003673168

Lewis, T. J., Mitchell, B. S., Harvey, K., Green, A., & McKenzie, J. (2015). A comparison of functional behavioral assessment and functional analysis methodology among students with mild disabilities. *Behavioral Disorders, 41*, 5–20. doi:10.17988/0198-7429-41.1.5

Lewis, T. J., & Sugai, G. (1996a). Functional assessment of problem behavior: A pilot investigation of the comparative and interactive effects of teacher and peer social attention on students in general education settings. *School Psychology Quarterly, 11*, 1–19. doi:10.1037/h0088918

Lewis, T. J., & Sugai, G. (1996b). Descriptive and experimental analysis of teacher and peer attention and the use of assessment based intervention to improve the pro-social behavior of a student in a general education setting. *Journal of Behavioral Education, 6*, 7–24. doi:10.1007/BF02110474

Liaupsin, C. J., Umbreit, J., Ferro, J. B., Urso, A., & Upreti, G. (2006). Improving academic engagement through systematic, function-based intervention. *Education and Treatment of Children, 29*, 573–591.

Losel, F., & Beelman, A. (2003). Effects of child skills training in preventing antisocial behavior: A systematic review of randomized evaluations. *Annals, AAPSS, 857*, 84–109. doi:10.1177/0002716202250793

Medland, M. B. & Stachnik, T. J. (1972). Good-behavior game: A replication and systematic analysis. *Journal of Applied Behavior Analysis, 5*, 45–51. doi:10.1901/jaba.1972.5-45

Mikami, A. Y., Jia, M., & Na, J. J. (2014) Social skills training. *Child and Adolescent Psychiatric Clinics of North America, 23*, 775–788. doi:10.1016/j.chc.2014.05.007

Nelson, J. R., & Roberts, M. L. (2000). Ongoing reciprocal teacher-student interactions involving disruptive behaviors in general education classrooms. *Journal of Emotional and Behavioral Disorders, 8*, 27–37. doi:10.1177/106342660000800104

Newcomer, L. L. & Lewis, T. J. (2004). Functional behavioral assessment: An investigation of assessment reliability and effectiveness of function-based interventions. *Journal of Emotional and Behavioral Disorders, 12*, 168–181. doi:10.1177/10634266040120030401

Northrup, J., Wacker, D., Sasso, G., Steege, M., Cigrand, K., Cook, J., & DeRaad, A. (1991). A brief functional analysis of aggressive and alternative behavior in an outpatient clinic setting. *Journal of Applied Behavior Analysis, 24*, 509–522. doi:10.1901/jaba.1991.24-509

Park, K. L., & Scott, T. M. (2009). Antecedent-based interventions for young children at risk for emotional and behavioral disorders. *Behavioral Disorders, 34*, 196–211.

Payne, L. D., Scott, T. M., & Conroy, M. (2007). A school-based examination of the efficacy of function-based intervention. *Behavioral Disorders, 32*, 158–174.

Quinn, M. M., Kavale, K. A., Mathur, S. R., Rutherford, R. B., & Forness, S. R. (1999). A meta-analysis of social skill interventions for students with emotional or behavioral disorders. *Journal of Emotional and Behavioral Disorders, 7*, 54–64. doi:10.1177/106342669900700106

Ryan, R., & Deci, E. (2000) Intrinsic and extrinsic motivations: Classic definitions and new directions. *Contemporary Educational Psychology 25*, 54–67. doi:10.1006/ceps.1999.1020

Scott, T. M., & Kamps, D. M. (2007). The future of functional behavioral assessment in school settings. *Behavioral Disorders, 32*, 146–157.

Simonsen, B., Fairbanks, S., Briesch, A., Myers, D., & Sugai, G. (2008). Evidence-based practices in classroom management: Considerations for research to practice. *Education and Treatment of Children, 31*, 351–380. doiL10.1353/etc.0.0007

Simonsen, B., & Myers, D. (2015). *Classwide positive behavior interventions and supports: A guide to proactive classroom management*. New York, NY: Guilford.

Simonsen, B., Myers, D., & DeLuca, C. (2010). Teaching teachers to use prompts, opportunities to respond, and specific praise. *Teacher Education and Special Education, 33*, 300–318. doi:10.1177/0888406409359905

Solnick, M. D., & Ardoin, S. P. (2010). A quantitative review of functional analysis procedures in public school settings. *Education and Treatment of Children, 33*, 153–175. doi:10.1353/etc.0.0083

Spencer, V. G., Scruggs, T. E., & Mastropieri, M. A. (2003). Content area learning in middle school social studies classrooms and students with emotional or behavioral disorders: A comparison of strategies. *Behavioral Disorders, 28*, 77–93.

Stichter, J., & Lewis, T. J. (2006). Classroom assessment: Targeting variables to improve instruction through a multi-level eco-behavioral model. In M. Hersen (Ed.), *Clinician's handbook of child behavioral assessment* (pp. 569–586). Burlington, MA: Elsevier.

Stichter, J. P., Lewis, T. J., Johnson, N., & Trussell, R. (2004). Toward a structural assessment: Analyzing the merits of an assessment tool for a student with E/BD. *Assessment for Effective Intervention, 30*, 25–40. doi:10.1177/073724770403000103

Stichter, J. P., Lewis, T. J., Whittaker, T. A., Richter, M., Johnson, N. W., & Trussell, R. P. (2009). Assessing teacher use of opportunities to respond and effective classroom management strategies: Comparisons among high- and low-risk elementary schools. *Journal of Positive Behavior Interventions, 11*, 68–81. DOI: 10.1177/1098300708326597

Sugai, G., & Lewis, T. (1996). Preferred and promising practices for social skill instruction. *Focus on Exceptional Children, 29*(4), 1–16.

Sutherland, K., Alder, V. & Gunter, P. (2003). The effect of varying rate of opportunities to respond to academic requests on the classroom behavior of students with EBD. *Journal of Emotional and Behavioral Disorders, 11*, 239–248. doi:10.1177/10634266030110040501

Sutherland, K., Wehby, J., & Copeland, S. (2000). Effect on varying rates of behavior-specific praise on the on-task behavior of students with EBD. *Journal of Emotional and Behavioral Disorders, 8*, 2–8. doi:10.1177/106342660000800101

Sutherland, K. S., Wehby, J. H., & Yoder, P. J. (2002). Examination of the relationship between teacher praise and opportunities for students with EBD to respond to academic requests. *Journal of Emotional and Behavioral Disorders, 10*, 5–13. doi:10.1177/106342660201000102

Stichter, J. P., Lewis, T. J., Whittaker, T. A., Richter, M., Johnson, N. W., & Trussell, R. P. (2009). Assessing teacher use of opportunities to respond and effective classroom management strategies: Comparisons among high- and low-risk elementary schools. *Journal of Positive Behavior Interventions, 11*, 68–81. doi:10.1177/1098300708326597

Umbreit, J. (1995). Functional assessment and intervention in a regular classroom setting for the disruptive behavior of a student with attention deficit hyperactivity disorder. *Behavioral Disorders, 20*, 267–278.

Wehby, J. H., Tally, B. B., & Falk, K. B. (2004). Identifying the relation between the function of problem behavior and teacher instructional behavior. *Assessment for Effective Instruction, 30*, 41–51. doi:10.1177/073724770403000104

What Works Clearinghouse. (2008, September). *Reducing behavior problems in the elementary school classroom: A practice guide* (NCEE #2008-012). Washington, DC: National Center for Education Evaluation and Regional Assistance, Institute of Education Sciences, U.S. Department of Education. Retrieved from http://ies.ed.gov/ncee/wwc/Docs/PracticeGuide/behavior_pg_092308.pdf

Wood, B. K., Blair, K. S., & Ferro, J. B. (2009). Young children with challenging behavior: Function-based assessment and intervention. *Topics in Early Childhood Special Education, 29*(2), 68–78. doi:10.1177/0271121409337951

Research Syntheses: Instruction

High-Leverage Practices

Teaching students with disabilities is a strategic, flexible, and recursive process as effective special education teachers use content knowledge, pedagogical knowledge (including evidence-based practice), and data on student learning to design, deliver, and evaluate the effectiveness of instruction. This process begins with well-designed instruction. Effective special education teachers are well versed in general education curricula and other contextually relevant curricula, and use appropriate standards, learning progressions, and evidence-based practices in conjunction with specific individualized education program (IEP) goals and benchmarks to prioritize long- and short-term learning goals and to plan instruction. This instruction, when delivered with fidelity, is designed to maximize academic learning time, actively engage learners in meaning-ful activities, and emphasize proactive and positive approaches across tiers of instructional intensity.

Effective special education teachers base their instruction and support of students with disabilities on the best available evidence, combined with their professional judgment and knowledge of individual student needs. Teachers value diverse perspectives and incorporate knowledge about students' backgrounds, culture, and language in their instructional decisions. Their decisions result in improved student outcomes across varied curriculum areas and in multiple educational settings. They use teacher-led, peer-assisted, student-regulated, and technology-assisted practices fluently, and know when and where to apply them. Analyzing instruction in this way allows teachers to improve student learning and their professional practice.

HLP11	Identify and prioritize long- and short-term learning goals.

Teachers prioritize what is most important for students to learn by providing meaningful access to and success in the general education and other contextually relevant curricula. Teachers use grade-level standards, assessment data and learning progressions, students' prior knowledge, and IEP goals and benchmarks to make decisions about what is most crucial to emphasize, and develop long- and short-term goals accordingly. They understand essential curriculum components, identify essential prerequisites and foundations, and assess student performance in relation to these components.

Special education teachers develop learning goals for students on a long- and short-term basis; these goals determine the focus of instruction. Learning goals include those for students' IEPs as well as for specific subjects (e.g., what to emphasize in math) or sub-areas (e.g., teaching particular concepts and skills in fractions, comprehension of expository text, linear measurement). In prioritizing these goals, teachers identify the most essential, powerful, equitable, and crucial learning outcomes. Multiple policy and practice factors influence this process.

The Individuals with Disabilities Education Act (IDEA, 2006) requires that IEP goals relate to the student's present level of academic achievement and functional performance (20 U.S.C § 1414 [d][1][A][i][I]), and that students with disabilities be provided access to the general education curriculum with appropriate accommodations (IDEA regulations, 2012, 34 C.F.R. § 300.39[3][ii]). Like IDEA, the Every Student Succeeds Act (ESSA; 2015), the successor to the No Child Left Behind Act of 2001, requires states to "promote the involvement" of students with disabilities, including those with significant cognitive disabilities, in the general education curriculum (U.S. Department of Education, 2016, p. 24). ESSA also

> imposed a cap to limit to 1.0 percent of the total student population the number of students with the most

significant cognitive disabilities to whom the State may administer an alternate assessment aligned with alternate academic achievement standards in each assessed subject area. (U.S. Department of Education, 2016, p. 2)

Thus, 99% of students with disabilities in a given population should take the statewide assessments or standards-based tests in each subject area.

Over 40 states and the District of Columbia have adopted the Common Core State Standards (CCSS). The CCSS "Applications to Students with Disabilities" document (CCSS Initiative, n.d.) clarifies the applicability of these standards to students with disabilities; states and districts have developed policies and procedures to link student IEP goals to the CCSS (e.g., Hanselman, 2013; Office of the Superintendent of Public Instruction & Washington Education Association, n.d.). School districts also disseminate pacing guides that identify what is to be taught in a grade, the sequence in which it should be taught, and a timeline (e.g., Tennessee Curriculum Center, 2011–2016).

Finally, there is extensive literature in special education about the need for and success of instruction in foundational skills (e.g. L. S. Fuchs et al., 2015; Moats, 2014; Vaughn, Danielson, Zumetta, & Holdheide,

2015; What Works Clearinghouse, 2009a), even though grade-level standards many not focus on them. All of these factors need to be considered when determining students' goals and objectives so that students with disabilities receive instruction in areas based on their specific strengths and needs while also being provided the maximum opportunity to meet the rigorous standards to which other students are held.

Research Support

In 2000, the National Reading Panel identified critical areas of reading instruction, and similar recommendations have been made for writing (e.g., Graham & Perin, 2007) and mathematics (e.g., U.S. Department of Education, 2008). The Institute for Education Sciences (IES) Practice Guides, based on research reviews using WWC guidelines, also make instructional recommendations. For example, the WWC Practice Guide for mathematics (2009b) recommended an in-depth focus on whole numbers in Grades K–5 and on rational numbers in Grades 4–8, noting that "fewer topics, in more depth, [is] more important for students who struggle with mathematics" (p. 18). Concerning primary students struggling in reading, the recommendation was to focus on up to three foundational skills (WWC, 2009a).

Another source of guidance is the identification of "big ideas," defined in mathematics as "a statement of an idea that is central to … learning…, one that links numerous mathematics into a coherent whole" (Charles, 2005, p.10). Learning progressions, or *developmental learning trajectories* (e.g., Consortium for Policy Research in Education, 2011; Heritage, 2009; Hess, 2011), also help teachers identify and select key prerequisites to teach, as does the scope and sequence of strong curriculum. L. S. Fuchs and colleagues (2015) studied the effect of a fraction intervention that reduced the range of topics and found students in the intervention group outperformed those who received instruction in the general education classroom, in several measures of fraction knowledge and skills. Although the researchers did not focus specifically on prioritizing goals, this research involved prioritizing what was taught (along with how it was taught)—in this case based on deep understanding of the domain. Intervention research such as this points to the importance of well-thought-out instructional focus areas.

Research addressing instruction with students with more severe intellectual disability also informs how teachers can prioritize learning goals. Browder and colleagues (2003), in a review of alternate assessment performance indicators, noted increased expectations for academic learning along with the need to address functional skills, communication and inclusion, and self-determination. Other studies (e.g., Collins, Hager, & Galloway, 2011; Karl, Collins, Hager, & Ault, 2013) have demonstrated the effectiveness of combining instruction in core content based on alternative standards with instruction in functional skills, rather than choosing between then.

> *Intervention research … points to the importance of well-thought-out instructional focus areas.*

Conclusion

Prioritized short- and long-term learning goals drive instruction, although grade-level standards and mandates for enabling students' access to the general education curriculum influence teachers' decisions about prioritizing. However, all standards are not of equal importance (Chard, n.d.); the same can be said of conceptual understandings and skills. In addition, there is a need for out-of-level instruction for some students (L. S. Fuchs et al., 2015); teachers need to identify and prioritize students' goals around critical content (Doabler et al., 2012) while linking to their present level of performance, strengths, and needs.

HLP12	Systematically design instruction toward a specific learning goal.

Teachers help students to develop important concepts and skills that provide the foundation for more complex learning. Teachers sequence lessons that build on each other and make connections explicit, in both planning and delivery. They activate students' prior knowledge and show how each lesson "fits" with previous ones. Planning involves careful consideration of learning goals, what is involved in reaching the goals, and allocating time accordingly. Ongoing changes (e.g., pacing, examples) occur throughout the sequence based on student performance.

Students with disabilities require more systematically designed instruction than their typically developing peers (Archer & Hughes, 2011). Researchers (e.g., Brophy & Good, 1986; Gersten, Schiller, & Vaughn, 2000; Marchand-Martella, Slocum, & Martella, 2004; Rosenshine & Stevens, 1986; Simmons, Fuchs, Fuchs, Mathes, & Hodge, 1995) have identified at least 16 elements of systematically designed instruction to include within and across lessons and units. Three elements—clear instructional goals, logical sequencing of knowledge and skills, and teaching students to organize content—are essential core components of systematic instruction.

Teachers design instruction that will help students meet challenging yet attainable learning goals that are stated clearly, concisely, and in measurable terms (Hattie, 2008). Instructional content is selected and sequenced logically to support or scaffold student learning. Less complex knowledge and skills are taught before more complex outcomes, information that is used frequently in the curriculum is taught prior to content that appears less often, prerequisites are mastered before higher level knowledge and skills, unambiguous information is taught before less clear material, and content and skills similar in form or function are taught separately before students are required to make independent discriminations among them (Archer & Hughes, 2011). Teachers make explicit connections among content and skills within and across lessons to allow students to link prior and new knowledge; see relationships among facts, concepts, and principles; and organize content to maximize retention, deepen understanding, and facilitate application.

Research Support

Hattie (2008) summarized findings from 11 meta-analyses on learning goals and concluded that achievement increases when teachers set specific challenging goals (rather than "do your best" goals) and structure learning activities so students can reach these goals. Overall effects varied and were highest when learning goals and success criteria were articulated and shared with students, and lowest when used for lesson planning.

L. S. Fuchs and Fuchs (1986) also noted that challenging goals were more effective for students with disabilities and reported effect sizes of $d = 0.63$ and $d = 0.67$ for long- and short-term goals, respectively. Klein, Wesson, Hollenbeck, and Alge (1999) found that, for students with disabilities, student commitment to goals was both helpful and necessary for learning.

Empirical support for well-sequenced lesson and unit design can be found in the literature relating to direct instruction (DI; Adams & Engelmann, 1996; Marchand-Martella et al., 2004). Hattie (2008) reviewed findings from four meta-analyses on DI and found an overall effect size of $d = 0.59$. Effects were similar for typically achieving students ($d = 0.99$) and those with or at risk for disabilities ($d = 0.86$), for word attack ($d = 0.64$) and comprehension ($d = 0.54$) skills, and for elementary and high school students. DI effects were higher for reading ($d = 0.89$) than for math ($d = 0.50$). Forness, Kavale, Blum, and Lloyd (1997) summarized findings from 18 meta-analyses on special education practices and found DI to be the only one of seven interventions to show strong evidence of effectiveness. The Best Evidence Encyclopedia (n.d.) has identified DI as one of six instructional practices with strong evidence of effectiveness.

Hattie (2008) also reviewed findings from 16 meta-analyses on the effects of visual content displays on student learning. Eleven meta-analyses on advance organizers produced a mean effect size of $d = 0.41$, and five meta-analyses on graphic organizers and concept maps produced an average effect size of $d = 0.57$. Effects were greater when instruction focused on central rather than detailed ideas (Nesbit & Adesope, 2006), displays were provided after initial content exposure (Moore & Readence, 1984), and students were provided terms for visual displays (Horton et al., 1993). Effect sizes were largest among students least likely to understand relationships between lower and higher order constructs (Horton et al., 1993; Kim, Vaughn, Wanzek, & Wei, 2004; Nesbit & Adesope, 2006; Vasquez & Caraballo, 1993) and mixed for teacher- versus student-generated displays (Kim et al., 2004; Nesbit & Adesope, 2006).

Although considerable research has been conducted on learning goals, lesson sequencing, and visual content displays, few studies have examined these practices in isolation.

Conclusion

Although considerable research has been conducted on learning goals, lesson sequencing, and visual content displays, few studies have examined these practices in isolation. As such, it is difficult to determine how much each practice contributes to overall intervention effectiveness. More systematic component analyses are needed (C. H. Kennedy, 2005). However, these practices are not likely to be applied in isolation; they usually are used collectively as part of well-designed lessons and units. Because even the best designed instruction may not result in satisfactory outcomes for all students, it is critical that student learning be monitored within and across lessons. If students are not making satisfactory progress, then inadequate lesson goals, poor lesson sequencing, or ambiguous connections might be examined as possible contributors.

HLP13	Adapt curriculum tasks and materials for specific learning goals.

Teachers assess individual student needs and adapt curriculum materials and tasks so that students can meet instructional goals. Teachers select materials and tasks based on student needs; use relevant technology; and make modifications by highlighting relevant information, changing task directions, and decreasing amounts of material. Teachers make strategic decisions on content coverage (i.e., essential curriculum elements), meaningfulness of tasks to meet stated goals, and criteria for student success.

Special education teachers select and adapt curriculum materials and tasks so students with disabilities can meet their IEP goals. Special educators make modifications by highlighting relevant information, changing task directions, and adjusting content amount and depth (Vaughn & Bos, 2012). Material adaptations can include

- making substitutions for text material (e.g., audiotaping content, reading content aloud, using other media, working individually with students),

- simplifying text (e.g., making abridged versions, providing outlines and summaries, using multilevel supports), and

- highlighting key concepts and information (e.g., previewing content, developing study guides, summarizing or reducing content).

Teachers may substitute text material when students are unable to read and extract information independently and simplify and highlight content to facilitate comprehension.

Special education teachers also use *content enhancements*, a range of strategies to augment the organization and delivery of curriculum content so that students can better access, interact with, understand, and retain information (Bulgren, 2006; Deshler et al., 2001). Three examples of specific enhancements are graphic organizers, guided notes, and mnemonics.

Graphic organizers are visual–spatial arrangements of information containing words or concepts connected graphically to help students see meaningful hierarchical, comparative, and sequential relationships (Dye, 2000; Ellis & Howard, 2007; Ives, 2007). There are numerous web-based resources teachers can use in developing and customizing graphic organizers for classroom use.

Guided notes are "teacher-prepared handouts that 'guide' a student through a lecture with standard cues and prepared space in which to write the key facts, concepts, and/or relationships" (Heward, 1994, p. 304). These are designed to actively engage students during teacher-led instruction and provide models of complete and accurate note-taking that can be used to prepare for academic assessments.

Mnemonics are memory-enhancing strategies that help students recall large amounts of unfamiliar information or make connections between two or more facts or concepts (Wolgemuth, Cobb, & Alwell, 2008). Three commonly used mnemonic techniques are letter strategies (Kleinheksel & Summy, 2003), the keyword method, and peg word strategies (Mastropieri & Scruggs, 2010). Again, numerous web-based resources (e.g., The Mnemonicizer and Spacefem's Mnemonic Generator) can help teachers create and customize mnemonics.

Research Support

Most empirical support for adapting curriculum materials and tasks is derived from research on graphic organizers, guided notes, and mnemonic strategies. Hattie (2008) reviewed findings from five meta-analyses on graphic organizers that produced an average effect size of $d = 0.57$. Instructional effects are greater when instruction focuses on the main idea rather than supporting details (Nesbit & Adesope, 2006), displays are provided after initial content exposure (Moore & Readence, 1984), and students are provided terms for visual displays (Horton et al., 1993). Kim and colleagues (2004) reported that graphic organizers improved comprehension performance for students with learning disabilities, effect sizes were larger for researcher-developed than for standardized measures, and initial gains in comprehension were not found on generalization or maintenance assessments. The use of graphic organizers has been rated as having a "strong level of evidence" by the National Technical Assistance Center on Transition (NTACT; 2016) and the Promising Practices Network, and received a "go for it" rating by the Council for Exceptional Children's (CEC) Current Practice Alerts (Ellis & Howard, 2007).

Numerous studies, including one meta-analysis (Konrad, Joseph, & Eveleigh, 2009), have found that guided notes improve students' academic performance on retention tests at grade levels from elementary through secondary and enhance students' note-taking accuracy (e.g., Hamilton, Seibert, Gardner, & Talbert-Johnson, 2000; Musti-Rao, Kroeger, & Schumaker-Dyle, 2008; Patterson, 2005; Sweeney et al., 1999). More

> It is difficult to assess the strength of research support for curricular and material adaptations per se because they are used for different purposes.

specifically, Konrad and colleagues (2009) reported that guided notes

- produced consistent, positive effects on students' academic performance and note-taking accuracy in Grades 4 through 12;
- had greater impact when supplemented with structured review activities (e.g., prompting questions, study guides and reflection questions, graphic organizers or other diagrams); and
- were particularly effective for students with disabilities when systematic training on their use was included.

In a meta-analysis examining the effects of mnemonics, Scruggs and Mastropieri (2000) reported that these memory-enhancing devices produced an unusually large mean effect size of 1.62 across 20 empirical studies, 19 of which involved students with learning disabilities. These findings were consistent with an earlier narrative review (Mastropieri, Scruggs, & Levin, 1985) that found that students receiving mnemonic instruction outperformed their peers on a variety of school learning tasks. A series of laboratory and field-based investigations (e.g., Scruggs & Mastropieri, 1989, 1991; Scruggs, Mastropieri, McLoone, Levin, & Morrison, 1987) showed similar positive effects for students with learning disabilities' academic performance in literacy, social studies, and science. NTACT (2016) and the Promising Practices Network have rated mnemonics as having a "strong level of evidence" for academic outcomes and CEC's Division for Learning Disabilities' Current Practice Alerts assigned mnemonics a "go for it" rating (Brigham & Brigham, 2001).

Conclusion

It is difficult to assess the strength of research support for curricular and material adaptations per se because they are used for different purposes (e.g., highlight important content, change task directions, adjust content amount and depth), include multiple instructional practices (e.g., graphic organizers, guided notes, mnemonic devices) that are used in isolation or together, and focus on individualized and ever-changing student outcomes. There does appear to be sufficient empirical support, however, for the three content enhancement approaches described here. Additional research must be conducted on the broader intervention "package" of making curricular and material adaptations. What kinds of adaptations are made, how are they implemented with fidelity, and what impact do they have on important student outcomes? Are some types of adaptations more effective, efficient, and socially acceptable than others? What are the active procedural components in these intervention packages (C. H. Kennedy, 2005)?

There is logical support for teachers to adapt instructional materials and tasks to support specific learning goals. By substituting, simplifying, and highlighting important instructional content, teachers increase the likelihood that students, including those with disabilities, will meet these learning goals. Although teachers understand the need to make adaptations to curriculum tasks and materials for students with disabilities, research also suggests that many fail to do so (e.g., Moody, Vaughn, & Schumm, 1997; Schumm, Moody, & Vaughn, 2000; Schumm & Vaughn, 1992; Schumm, Vaughn & Saumell, 1992). Thus, attention should be focused on the actual implementation of instructional modifications and their subsequent effect on student outcomes.

HLP14	Teach cognitive and metacognitive strategies to support learning and independence.

Teachers explicitly teach cognitive and metacognitive processing strategies to support memory, attention, and self-regulation of learning. Learning involves not only understanding content but also using cognitive processes to solve problems, regulate attention, organize thoughts and materials, and monitor one's own thinking. Self-regulation and metacognitive strategy instruction is integrated into lessons on academic content through modeling and explicit instruction. Students learn to monitor and evaluate their performance in relation to explicit goals and make necessary adjustments to improve learning.

Because students with disabilities do not typically use learning strategies to improve academic performance like their typically developing peers do, they must be taught explicitly to use strategies. Strategies are not step-by-step instructions; instead, a *strategy* "is a heuristic that supports or facilitates the learner" in using higher order thinking or skills (Rosenshine & Meister, 1992, p. 26). Newell (1990) noted that there are two layers of problem solving when using strategies: applying a strategy to a problem, and selecting and monitoring the effects of that strategy. Cognitive strategies (e.g., making predictions, summarizing, apply grammar rules, making meaning from context) are representative of the former, whereas metacognitive strategies (e.g., self-management and self-regulation, planning and monitoring) depict the latter. Strategies help students become "proficient problem solvers" (Montague & Dietz, 2009, p. 286) by teaching them how to self-monitor learning or behavior, recognize problem areas, create and execute solutions, and evaluate success. In short, cognitive strategy instruction teaches students how to learn (Jitendra, Burgess, & Gajria, 2011).

Strategies go across content and skill areas. Some examples of common cognitive strategies include:

- for reading comprehension, collaborative strategic reading (Vaughn et al., 2011) and text interaction strategies (e.g., summarizing, text structure, identifying main idea; Jitendra et al., 2011);

- for writing, the self-regulated strategy development (SRSD) model (Harris & Graham, 2003; Santangelo, Harris, & Graham, 2008);

- for mathematics, enhanced anchored instruction (Bottge et al., 2015), Solve It (Krawec, Huang, Montague, Kressler, & de Alba, 2013), and schema-based instruction (Jitendra & Star, 2011);

- for retention and memory, keyword mnemonic strategies and letter strategies (Fontana, Scruggs, & Mastropieri, 2007); and

- for self-management, self-monitoring (Bruhn, McDaniel, & Kreigh, 2015) and SLANT (Ellis, 1991).

These strategies are effectively taught through explicit instruction, including structured and organized lessons, modeling, guided practice, progress monitoring, and feedback (Archer & Hughes, 2011). In the modeling stage, students observe the teacher using the strategy while thinking aloud to demonstrate how skilled problem solvers approach tasks. Think-alouds also help students build their metacognitive ability (i.e., the ability to think about their thinking; Montague & Dietz, 2009).

Research Support

The vast majority of the research on cognitive strategy instruction has been conducted since the late 1990s. Researchers have developed new strategies (some of which are listed above) and conducted empirical studies to determine their impact on student achievement. Meta-analyses on these strategies have found that as a whole they are strongly effective, and researchers in many different fields have concluded that strategy instruction is an evidence-based practice for students with disabilities (see Cook & Cook, 2013, for criteria for determining evidence-based practices).

In a synthesis of the quality of studies on cognitive strategy instruction in mathematics, Montague and Dietz (2009) found that the collected studies did not meet the recommendations for identifying evidence-based practices, but the authors noted that the reviewed studies all showed positive and promising results for students. Jitendra et al. (2011) conducted a meta-analysis of studies on cognitive strategy instruction for expository texts and found two group design studies that met the criteria for high quality and two that met the criteria for acceptable quality. The effect sizes calculated based on these studies were 1.12 (high only) and 1.26 (all four), which were both significantly different from 0. Based on this, Jitendra and colleagues concluded that cognitive strategy instruction was an evidence-based practice for teaching students with disabilities to comprehend expository text. In a meta-analysis of science instruction for students with disabilities, Kaldenberg, Watt, and Therrien (2015) found a related moderate effect size of .64 for reading comprehension strategies (e.g., using a graphic organizer, text structure).

Two different meta-analyses on writing instruction for students with disabilities have found moderate to strong weighted effect sizes for strategy instruction: .82 (Graham & Perin, 2007), and 1.09 (Gillespie & Graham, 2014). Other researchers have found that SRSD alone definitely meets the criteria and is an evidence-based practice (Baker, Chard, Ketterlin-Geller, Apichatabutra, & Doabler, 2009). Finally, Hattie (2008) provided effect sizes for a number of cognitive and metacognitive strategies that ranged from .22 (environmental restructuring) to .85 (organizing and transforming materials).

Conclusion

Cognitive strategy instruction and metacognitive strategy instruction encompasses a range of instructional techniques designed to help students become more self-directed and independent learners. These strategies, when taught explicitly with modeling and guided practice, have been proven effective in multiple studies across content areas and disability types.

HLP15	Provide scaffolded supports.

Scaffolded supports provide temporary assistance to students so they can successfully complete tasks that they cannot yet do independently and with a high rate of success. Teachers select powerful visual, verbal, and written supports; carefully calibrate them to students' performance and understanding in relation to learning tasks; use them flexibly; evaluate their effectiveness; and gradually remove them once they are no longer needed. Some supports are planned prior to lessons and some are provided responsively during instruction.

Scaffolded supports are supports provided to students that are either preplanned or provided "on the spot" and then faded or removed once they are not needed (Rosenshine, 2012); teachers gradually release or transfer responsibility to students (Pearson & Gallagher, 1983) as they become more proficient. Scaffolded supports can be provided in multiple forms including dialogue (e.g., modeling, hints, questions, partial completion of the task, informative feedback; Englert, Tarrant, Mariage, & Oxer, 1994; Palincsar & Brown, 1984), materials (e.g., cue cards, anchor charts, checklists, models of completed tasks; Rosenshine, 2012; Rosenshine & Meister, 1992), and technology (Putambecker & Hübscher, 2005). The term *scaffolded instruction* was introduced by Wood, Bruner, and Ross (1976) based on their study of parent–child interactions and defined by them as assistance by adults that "enables a child or novice to solve a problem, carry out a task or achieve a goal which would be beyond his unassisted efforts" (p. 90). Scaffolding occurs within Vygotsky's *zone of proximal development* (1978)–the distance between what a child can understand and do independently and what he or she can understand and do with assistance. Special education teachers use effective supports for student learning; to do so, the teacher must fully understand the task as well as students' changing understanding and proficiency. For example,

- A middle-school teacher makes an Accountable Talk chart, consisting of sentence stems that students can use in discussions. She and another teacher model a discussion using the stems; students then use these stems in their contributions to the discussion, and later rate themselves using an Accountable Talk scorecard (T. V. Mariage, personal communication, May 15, 2016).

- A primary teacher, in talking to his students during writing instruction, uses step-in moves and step-back moves (Englert & Dunsmore, 2002) during writing instruction. If the students struggle, the teacher steps in—modeling, thinking aloud; once students develop more confidence and proficiency, he steps back, letting the children complete the writing on their own.

Research Support

Scaffolded supports are often a component of instructional "packages," or instructional interventions that involve multiple components. Several effective reading comprehension instructional approaches incorporate scaffolded supports, with reciprocal teaching (Palincsar, 1986; Palincsar & Brown, 1984) perhaps the most prominent example. The What Works Clearinghouse (2010b) identified six studies of reciprocal teaching that met its standard; this research showed medium to large gains in reading comprehension for adolescents when using reciprocal teaching. Hattie (2008), reviewing two meta-analyses of reciprocal teaching, found high effect sizes on comprehension achievement. Comprehension gains associated with reciprocal teaching have been seen with struggling students with

disabilities (e.g., Gajria, Jitendra, Sood & Sacks, 2007; Klingner & Vaughn, 1996; Lederer, 2000).

Scaffolding is a strong component in other instructional packages such as collaborative strategic reading (Klingner, Vaughn, Dimino, Schumm & Bryant, 2001) and POSSE (Englert & Mariage, 1991). Boardman, Swanson, Klingner, and Vaughn's (2013) review of collaborative strategic reading experimental and quasi-experimental studies found gains in reading comprehension for students with learning disabilities. Englert and Mariage (1991) found that fourth-, fifth-, and sixth-grade students with learning disabilities recalled significantly more ideas and produced better organized written recalls, as well as had more strategy knowledge, than students in the control group after participating in POSSE. SRSD (Graham, Harris & Mason, 2005), as part of a writing instruction package, involves substantial teacher scaffolding. Both group planning and single-subject studies (reviewed by Mason, Harris & Graham 2011) showed that SRSD had positive effects on aspects of writing such as quality, planning, and revising in students across disability areas. Finally, scaffolded supports are incorporated into learning routines in content enhancement routines. Lenz and Bulgren's (2013) review of the research surrounding content enhancement routines found positive effects for factual and conceptual comprehension. Other scaffolded instructional "packages" include tools such as cue cards or strategy sheets (e.g., Englert & Mariage, 1991; Klingner et al., 2001), routines with mnemonics (Mason, Harris & Graham, 2011), graphic organizers (e.g., Jitendra, 2007; Lenz & Bulgren, 2013), and checklists (e.g., Jitendra, 2007; Mason et al., 2011), so it is difficult to identify the exact contribution of each component.

Researchers have also looked at individual scaffolded supports. For example, Gajria and colleagues (2007) reviewed 11 studies of content enhancers including semantic mapping, advance organizers, and mnemonic illustrations, and concluded that there was strong support for using these scaffolds to aid comprehension of content by students with learning disabilities. Similarly, Dexter and Hughes (2011) reviewed studies that showed the effect of graphic organizers on factual comprehension of content by students with learning disabilities in upper elementary, middle, and high schools. E. Swanson and colleagues' (2014) meta-analysis of reading interventions including mnemonics, graphic organizers, and guided notes showed positive effects on content and comprehension of students with learning disabilities and improvement in vocabulary and inference/relational comprehension. It is unclear from these meta-analyses, however, whether the supports were faded when students were successful, and how support was adjusted.

Conclusion

Although it is difficult to isolate the specific contribution of scaffolded supports, they are a key component of instructional approaches that have been shown to increase student performance. Grounded in theory that stresses interactions, ongoing assessment, and fading of support as students become more independent, scaffolded supports occur in many forms. Providing scaffolded supports—both those that are preplanned and those that occur "on the spot"—and removing them when students no longer need them is an important and powerful teaching practice.

HLP16	Use explicit instruction.

Teachers make content, skills, and concepts explicit by showing and telling students what to do or think while solving problems, enacting strategies, completing tasks, and classifying concepts. Teachers use explicit instruction when students are learning new material and complex concepts and skills. They strategically choose examples and non-examples and language to facilitate student understanding, anticipate common misconceptions, highlight essential content, and remove distracting information. They model and scaffold steps or processes needed to understand content and concepts, apply skills, and complete tasks successfully and independently.

Explicit instruction (EI) is a direct, structured, supportive, and systematic methodology for teaching academic skills (Archer & Hughes, 2011). When using EI, the teacher provides an explanation or model, guides students through application of the skill or concept, and provides opportunities for independent application of the skill or concept to ensure mastery (Mercer, Mercer, & Pullen, 2011).

EI allows teachers to use research-based underlying principles of effective instruction, active student engagement, promoting high levels of success, increasing content coverage, instructional grouping, scaffolding instruction, and addressing different forms of knowledge (Ellis & Worthington, 1994). Rosenshine (1983) developed a list of six fundamental teaching functions that incorporate principles of explicit instruction: review, presenting new content in small steps, using guided practice, providing corrective feedback, providing independent practice (both massed and distributed), and weekly/monthly cumulative reviews. When teachers use EI, academic learning time increases, which is strongly linked to student achievement (Archer & Hughes, 2011). In essence, explicit instruction is a set of teacher behaviors that have repeatedly shown to have a positive impact on student achievement, especially those who are struggling to learn.

Research Support

Teacher effect studies have been conducted on the use of EI elements from various perspectives including reading research, general and special education, cognitive science, and brain imaging studies, all of which have provided converging support for the practice. In addition, EI has been shown to help students learn a variety of academic and academically related skills. For example, EI has been used to successfully teach language skills such as vocabulary (Coyne, Simmons, Kame'enui, & Stoolmiller, 2004; Pullen, Tuckwiller, Konold, Maynard, & Coyne, 2010), word recognition skills in reading (Connor, Jakobsons, Crowe, & Meadows, 2009; Moats, 2000; Stanovich, 1994), and writing strategies (Harris & Graham, 1996; Harris, Graham, & Mason, 2003). Vaughn, Gersten, and Chard (2000)

> *Explicit instruction is a set of teacher behaviors that have repeatedly shown to have a positive impact on student achievement, especially those who are struggling to learn.*

analyzed 13 studies in writing instruction and concluded that EI represents best practice in teaching steps in the writing process and teaching writing conventions. EI also has shown to be effective for students who are struggling to learn math skills and concepts (L. S. Fuchs et al., 2008; Good, Grouws, & Ebmeier, 1983). The National Mathematics Advisory Panel (U.S. Department of Education, 2008) also supports using explicit instruction to teach computation and problem-solving skills. Finally, EI has been effective in teaching students a variety of cognitive learning strategies to help them become more independent learners (Hughes, 2011)

Conclusion

Explicit instruction is an effective as well as efficient methodology for teaching students (Archer & Hughes, 2011). The elements of EI are clearly operationalized and are based on a wide range of empirical studies spanning more than 40 years. These elements address principles of EI when designing and delivering instruction. When EI is used in the classroom, academic learning time is increased. Evidence supports the use of EI with all students (in both general and special education settings), across all ages and grade levels, and across content areas. EI can be used with all learners but is essential for struggling learners. Novice teachers can master the methodology and skillfully use this HLP to teach all learners effectively.

HLP17	Use flexible grouping.

Teachers assign students to homogeneous and heterogeneous groups based on explicit learning goals, monitor peer interactions, and provide positive and corrective feedback to support productive learning. Teachers use small learning groups to accommodate learning differences, promote in-depth academic-related interactions, and teach students to work collaboratively. They choose tasks that require collaboration, issue directives that promote productive and autonomous group interactions, and embed strategies that maximize learning opportunities and equalize participation. Teachers promote simultaneous interactions, use procedures to hold students accountable for collective and individual learning, and monitor and sustain group performance through proximity and positive feedback.

Special education teachers use flexible grouping to differentiate instruction and meet individual student needs. Grouping patterns change often depending on lesson goals and objectives and may include (a) homogeneous and heterogeneous small groups, (b) pairs, (c) whole class, and (d) individual instruction (Hoffman, 2002; Vaughn & Bos, 2012). Varied grouping arrangements are used flexibly to accommodate learning differences, promote in-depth academic-related interactions, and teach students to work collaboratively. Numerous professional organizations (e.g., International Literacy Association, 2010; National Board for Professional Teaching Standards, 2016) support the use of flexible grouping. Within flexible grouping, many special educators effectively use small groups (i.e., two to six students) to provide focused, intensive instruction. Special education teachers must be skilled in using both *homogeneous* (same-ability) and *heterogeneous* (mixed-ability) small groups to help students meet explicit learning goals.

Homogeneous groups are used to provide focused, intensive instruction for students with common instructional strengths and needs and are configured to meet short-term goals and objectives

(Cohen & Lotan, 2014). Special education teachers first identify a limited number of high-priority skills and concepts (i.e., big ideas) and form small instructional groups of students with similar academic abilities and needs. They then provide explicit instruction (i.e., modeling, guided and independent practice) for relatively short time periods and use strategies to maximize student response opportunities (e.g., additional time allocations, rapid pacing, unison responding practices), increase instructional feedback, and monitor student progress. To maximize instructional intensity, teachers use smaller group sizes; for example, a group of one to two students has been found most effective for improving achievement (Erlbaum, Vaughn, Hughes, & Moody, 2000; Iverson, Tunmer, & Chapman, 2005; Vaughn et al., 2003). Teachers may also provide additional time allocations to ensure student mastery (McLesky & Waldron, 2011).

Heterogeneous groups include students of varied knowledge and skill levels and can serve multiple instructional purposes. Special education teachers use small, mixed-ability groups to engage all students in grade-level content-related conversations, facilitate student thinking and communication skills, and improve interpersonal relationships among students with and without disabilities (Hattie, 2008; Kagan & Kagan, 2009). To use heterogeneous groups as intended, teachers initially form small groups (two to six members) who differ on demographic (i.e., gender, race, socioeconomic status, disability status) or academic-related (i.e., high, average, low achieving) variables. They then select tasks and materials that require collaboration (e.g., one material set), provide directives to promote productive and autonomous interactions, and embed strategies to maximize and equalize student response opportunities (e. g., structured and reciprocal student roles). Teachers monitor small-group interactions, provide positive and corrective feedback, hold students accountable individually and collectively, and sustain group interactions through proximity and feedback.

Research Support

The evidence base on small-group instruction—homogeneous and heterogeneous—is large, varies in rigor, and extends across multiple, related topics (e.g., ability grouping, intensive instruction, peer-mediated instruction, group contingencies, cooperative learning). Research support for the use of small, homogeneous groups can be found, for example, in literature on effective schools (Taylor, Pearson, Clark, & Walpole, 2000; Wharton-McDonald, Pressley, & Hampton, 1998), response to intervention (RTI; (Gersten et al., 2009; McMaster, Fuchs, Fuchs, & Compton, 2005), and preschool literacy (Connor et al., 2009; C. B. Jones, Reutzel, & Smith, 2012). Effective schools researchers reported that children in schools that used small, homogeneous groups had stronger reading skills than peers from schools that did not; preschool reading instruction in small groups produced main achievement effects; and small group gains were greater than similar instruction provided to the whole class. Small homogeneous, skill-based groups are also central to the three-tiered, RTI model for reading intervention (Al Otaiba & Fuchs, 2002; Coyne, Kame'enui, & Simmons, 2001) and are more prevalent in classrooms of highly effective than less effective teachers (i.e., 48 versus 25 minutes per day; C. B. Jones et al., 2012; Taylor et al., 2000).

Most research on small, heterogeneous groups is found in the cooperative learning literature and includes multiple meta-analyses to support its systematic application (e.g., Hattie, 2008; Johnson & Johnson, 1987, 2002; Johnson, Johnson, & Maruyama, 1983; Johnson, Maruyama, Johnson, Nelson, & Skon, 1981; Slavin, 1987, 1990). Hattie (2008) summarized findings that included 306 empirical studies, produced 829 effects, and involved over 24,000 individuals. Meta-analyses compared the effects of individualistic, competitive, and cooperative learning conditions on academic, behavioral, and interpersonal outcomes. Under *individualistic conditions*, students earn rewards based solely on their individual performance; in *competitive conditions*, they garner rewards by outperforming other group members (i.e., earn highest score); under *cooperative conditions*, students share rewards based on their collective group performance. Meta-analyses yielded moderate effect sizes of .59 (vs. individualistic) and .54 (vs. competitive) in favor of cooperative arrangements. Hattie reported further that cooperative learning effects (a) were higher in some

> *Researchers have reported that children in schools that used small, homogeneous groups had stronger reading skills than peers from schools that did not.*

subjects than others (e.g., reading, d = 0.44 vs. math, d = 0.01), (b) increased with age (elementary, d = 0.28, vs. middle school, d = 0.33, vs. high school, d = 0.43), and (c) were largest when individual accountability and group rewards were used (Stevens & Slavin, 1990).

Conclusion

It is difficult to assess the strength of the evidence base on flexible grouping per se because it involves the use of multiple instructional arrangements (i.e., from individual to whole group instruction) that are applied flexibly, often for short durations, and to meet individualized and ever-changing learning goals. Flexible grouping resembles an intervention package whose individual contributions to student success must be isolated and studied through component analyses (C. H. Kennedy, 2005). More empirical studies are needed to examine the decision-making process that undergirds the use of flexible grouping.

Both homogeneous and heterogeneous small-group arrangements, when well designed and implemented, can improve a variety of academic and interpersonal student outcomes (Hattie, 2008; Heward & Wood, 2015). Most evidence suggests that small groups should be highly structured and include (a) systematic goal, task, and material selection; (b) clear instructional directives; and (c) explicit strategies to maximize and equalize student response opportunities. Like all instructional practices, teachers must monitor student academic and interpersonal performance, provide positive and constructive feedback, and hold students accountable for their own and others' performance.

HLP18	Use strategies to promote active student engagement.

Teachers use a variety of instructional strategies that result in active student responding. Active student engagement is critical to academic success. Teachers must initially build positive student–teacher relationships to foster engagement and motivate reluctant learners. They promote engagement by connecting learning to students' lives (e. g., knowing students' academic and cultural backgrounds) and using a variety of teacher-led (e.g., choral responding and response cards), peer-assisted (e. g., cooperative learning and peer tutoring), student-regulated (e.g., self-management), and technology-supported strategies shown empirically to increase student engagement. They monitor student engagement and provide positive and constructive feedback to sustain performance.

Student engagement lies at the heart of positive academic outcomes. The correlation between student engagement and academic achievement is consistently strong and significant (Brophy, 1986; Rosenshine, 1976). Teachers frequently and flexibly use engagement strategies to motivate students and create personal connections; these strategies help students value their education and develop autonomy and interest in learning tasks. Engagement strategies ensure students are active participants in the learning process and school environment. Strategies may include group (i.e. cooperative learning groups, peer-assisted learning) or individually focused structures (e.g., personalized positive feedback, enlisting strategies). In addition to strategies to increase participation, teachers use strategies to connect learning to student's lives and increase students' value of and interest in school and feelings of belonging.

Student engagement is a multidimensional construct comprising cognitive, affective, and behavioral dimensions that are dynamic and responsive to teacher behavior. Therefore, a student's participation in school and class activities (*behavioral engagement*), feeling of belonging and value (*affective engagement*) and persistence and effort on difficult tasks (*cognitive engagement*) work together to define the level of engagement (REL Southeast, 2011). These dimensions are affected by teachers' behavior and instructional practices, which are central to active engagement and achievement in the classroom (Hattie, 2008; Scott, Hirn & Alter, 2014; Skinner & Belmont, 1993).

Engagement strategies should be strategically chosen and integrated into daily classroom instruction by special education teachers.

A student's level of engagement in school is a critical factor in that student's academic achievement and likelihood of graduating from high school. Students with disabilities, now often included in general education settings (McLeskey, Landers, Williamson, & Hoppey, 2012), may not actively participate or display as high engagement as their typically developing peers (Furlong, Morrison, & Dear, 1994; Hemmeter, Santos, & Ostrosky, 2008). In addition, students with disabilities are at greater risk of dropping out, and engagement is the greatest predictor of high school dropout (Dunn, Chambers & Rabren, 2004). By helping students set personal goals, explicitly teaching and modeling active engagement and participation behaviors,

and building positive relationships with students early in their academic career, many of the negative outcomes that place these students at risk can be prevented. Therefore, engagement strategies should be strategically chosen and integrated into daily classroom instruction by special education teachers.

Research Support

Student engagement is a strong predictor of academic achievement and behavior regardless of socioeconomic status or other student-level factors (Klem & Connell, 2009). Engaged and successful students are more likely to graduate from high school, whereas students who experience and disengagement eventually drop out (Appleton, Christenson, & Furlong, 2008; Archambault, Janosz, Morizot, & Pagani 2009; Christenson, Sinclair, Lehr, & Godber, 2001; Christenson & Thurlow, 2004; Rumberger, 2011). Marzano and Pickering's (2011) model of engagement organizes the essential components of engaging students around four questions that reflect the student's perspective:

How do I feel? Student enthusiasm, enjoyment, and pride (among other emotions) increase student engagement (Skinner, Kindermann, & Furrer, 2008). Students need an environment where they feel safe and supported in order to engage in academic tasks. Students' feelings of acceptance also play a role in their level of engagement. To address this, teachers:

- Ensure equity and fairness in academic opportunities including responding to questions, receiving rigorous material, and playing games (Marzano & Pickering, 2011).

- Design the learning environment to encourage active student participation and attention (e.g. table and desk arrangement, group size, location of instruction).

- Build positive personal relationships with students (e.g., know students' academic and cultural backgrounds; include students' names in instruction, examples, and text such as word problems; connect instruction to students' interests; Hattie, 2008).

- Provide positive feedback for students who are actively engaged and attentive (Hattie, 2008).

Am I interested? Student interest and choice is needed for students to be motivated and have ownership in their learning. Teachers:

- Incorporate student interest, choice, and physical movement (Dwyer, Blizzard & Dean, 1996; Dwyer, Sallis, Blizzard, Lazarus & Dean, 2001; Jensen, 2013).

- Keep the momentum of instruction and lesson pace appropriate for the attentional needs of students, including smooth transitions, effective use of instructional time, and effectively preparing students for independent tasks and activities (Emmer & Gerwels, 2006; Kubesch et al., 2009).

Is this important? Students must feel that what they are learning is worthwhile. Teachers need to be explicit in their instructional objectives and relate new information to knowledge students currently have.

Can I do this? Self-efficacy is necessary for a student to put forth effort and persist through difficult tasks. Students need to feel challenged and supported in order to attend to and complete tasks. Teachers:

- Have an awareness of students who are chronically disengaged and make

an effort to build relationship and use strategies to enlist students (e.g., teacher helper, mentoring, lunch buddies, encouragement; Archambault et al., 2009; Appleton et al., 2008; Christenson et al., 2001).

- Develop mastery measures for students to work towards, which is particularly important for students with disabilities who often are functioning on a different academic level than their same-age peers.

Effective student engagement practices hinge on the presence of positive teacher–student relationships and a climate that fosters community, ownership, and identity (Cornelius-White & Harbaugh, 2010; Jensen, 2013). Through his meta-analysis, Hattie (2008) found that teacher–student relationships has a substantial (0.72) effect size related to student achievement. Many other researchers have supported this finding (see Jackson, 2015). Hamre and Pianta (2006) emphasized the developmental nature of student engagement, finding that strong student-teacher relationships in kindergarten have robust effects on students' school outcomes lasting through eighth grade.

Conclusion

Drawing from the larger body of student engagement research in general education, the effect of student engagement is clear, especially for students at risk of poor learning outcomes. Though there is limited research on student engagement among students with disabilities, these students are at greater risk of dropping out than students without disabilities. Knowing that withdrawal and school disengagement lead to negative outcomes (Finn, 1993; Finn & Cox, 1992), teachers need to have multiple strategies to engage students with disabilities. It is particularly important for teachers in inclusive settings to be aware of the signs of disengagement and to employ strategies to interrupt the pattern of disengagement. To support the engagement of students with disabilities, early, positive, and consistent student engagement strategies should be used to promote favorable academic and behavioral outcomes.

HLP19	Use assistive and instructional technologies.

Teachers select and implement assistive and instructional technologies to support the needs of students with disabilities. They select and use augmentative and alternative communication devices and assistive and instructional technology products to promote student learning and independence. They evaluate new technology options given student needs; make informed instructional decisions grounded in evidence, professional wisdom, and students' IEP goals; and advocate for administrative support in technology implementation. Teachers use the universal design for learning (UDL) framework to select, design, implement, and evaluate important student outcomes.

Technology intended to support students with disabilities can be characterized as either *assistive* or *instructional* (M. J. Kennedy & Deshler, 2010). Assistive technology (AT) encompasses most examples of augmentative and assistive communication devices (AACs) that provide students with access to instruction. Other examples of AT include simple pencil grips, text-to-speech features, and advanced tools that help students who are nonverbal communicate with the outside world. AT is often personalized, thereby meeting an individual's specific need and mitigating the impact of the disability to enhance access to instruction, improve communication, support moving around, or otherwise enable individuals to participate in their world (Billingsley, Brownell, Israel, & Kamman, 2013). Instructional technologies are products and approaches intended to support student learning and engagement (e.g., learning-oriented games and software, instructional videos). Special education teachers often use assistive and instructional technologies in combination to address students' unique needs (Alper & Raharinirina, 2006).

Policy and Research Support

Technology plays a key role in the lives of students with disabilities (Israel, Marino, Delisio, & Serianni, 2014). Since the 1997 reauthorization of IDEA, IEP teams have been required to "consider whether the child requires assistive technology devices and services" (34 C.F.R. § 300.346[2][v]). When discussing the role of technology for supporting individualized needs for students with disabilities, it is appropriate to consider the promise of universal design for learning (UDL) for designing and delivering high quality instruction (Basham & Marino, 2013; Rao, Ok, & Bryant, 2014). More recently, ESSA referenced universal design for learning (UDL) as a framework that should be considered when designing and delivering instruction and assessments for all students (see CAST, 2016). UDL is a broad framework that guides a teacher to consider multiple means of representation, engagement, and expression when writing lesson plans, delivering instruction, and evaluating learning (Rose, Meyer, & Hitchcock, 2005). When teachers plan lessons using the UDL framework, they consider the interactions between students' needs and the content being taught.

It is challenging for empirical research to keep up with the rapid changes and improvements in technology. Promising tools often become obsolete too quickly for them to be thoroughly studied (Edyburn, 2013). Although there is an empirical base of literature surrounding technology for students with disabilities, it has been characterized as "scattershot" (Okolo & Bahr, 1995; Okolo & Bouck, 2007) and lacks a programmatic focus across and within studies. However, three types of technology for students with disabilities have received more attention from researchers: video self-modeling, augmentative and alternative communication systems (AACs), and computer-aided instruction.

Students with disabilities benefit when they have access to assistive technology devices and services.

Video self-modeling involves recording video of a student doing an activity and editing it to show only the segment in which the student meets the target performance goal or exhibits a target behavior. The student watches the clip prior to engaging in similar tasks. Prater, Carter, Hitchcock, and Dowrick's (2012) review of studies revealed that video self-modeling significantly improved performance on a variety of tasks, including reading fluency, on-task behavior, and arithmetic. Improvements in almost all cases (except writing skills) were maintained past the intervention phase.

Two examples of technology-based AACs are picture exchange communication systems and voice output communication aids. These devices are designed to aid communication for students who are nonverbal or cannot use conventional verbal language. In a meta-analysis of single case studies on the efficacy of AACs, Ganz and colleagues (2012) determined that AACs have strong effects for communication skills, social skills, academics, and challenging behaviors, with the strongest effects for communication skills.

Computer-aided instruction is instruction presented using a computer. When designed well, it can reduce the cognitive load on learners and increase their attention level, allowing for more efficient and effective learning (Mayer, 2008). A meta-analysis of studies on the use of computer-aided instruction to improve students' cognitive skills (e.g., perception, memory, attention) found a moderately positive effect with a weighted average effect size of .35 (Weng, Maeda, & Bouck, 2014).

Conclusion

Students with disabilities benefit when they have access to assistive technology devices and services, and when teachers use instructional technology to support their unique needs. In the future, technology will only accelerate in terms of affecting all students' daily lives, in and out of school. As a result, school professionals will be faced with increasingly important decisions regarding how to allocate resources when selecting, implementing, and evaluating the effects of various technology options (Okolo & Bouck, 2007). Thus, an important role for special education teachers is to stay abreast of technology developments and work with their school or district technology specialists to ensure the most effective use of assistive and instructional technologies to meet the needs of students with disabilities (Israel et al., 2014; S. J. Smith & Okolo, 2010).

HLP20	Provide intensive instruction.

Teachers match the intensity of instruction to the intensity of the student's learning and behavioral challenges. Intensive instruction involves working with students with similar needs on a small number of high priority, clearly defined skills or concepts critical to academic success. Teachers group students based on common learning needs; clearly define learning goals; and use systematic, explicit, and well-paced instruction. They frequently monitor students' progress and adjust their instruction accordingly. Within intensive instruction, students have many opportunities to respond and receive immediate, corrective feedback with teachers and peers to practice what they are learning.

In a schoolwide tiered system of support, the highest level of support is intensive intervention. Typically, this level of intervention, commonly referred to as Tier 3, is delivered by special educators, whereas supplemental intervention (Tier 2) is typically delivered by highly trained general educators. Tier 3 instruction is delivered through a process of data-based individualization (DBI). Through DBI, teachers start with a validated supplemental intervention and use diagnostic and ongoing progress monitoring data to design highly individualized instruction and continually adapt the intervention and instruction in response to student performance (National Center on Intensive Intervention, 2013). These instructional adaptations comprise *intensive instruction*. Tier 2 supplemental instruction also uses a research-based intervention to address skill gaps for students below grade level and not making progress with differentiated core instruction. Tier 2 instruction is delivered to small, homogeneous groups of students (approximately four to seven students) and aims to address skills that are foundational to accessing grade-level content, in order to prevent further academic failure.

Tier 3 intensive instruction is highly individualized for students with severe and persistent learning needs who, according to data, have not responded to evidence-based core instruction and supplemental intervention. Teachers incorporate evidence-based practices that have been proven effective for students with disabilities across all content areas including math, reading, writing and behavior. Intensive instruction integrates cognitive processing strategies; is explicit; integrates opportunities for feedback; and is responsive to student performance data (Baker, Gersten, & Lee, 2002; Santangelo, Harris, & Graham, 2007). Instruction is delivered to a small number of students (no more than three) with similar learning or behavioral needs (WWC, 2009a). Teachers group students based on common learning needs; clearly define learning goals; and use systematic, explicit, and well-paced instruction to address skill gaps.

Teachers use data to identify skills gaps and deliver instruction that is highly focused. Students are taught a small number of high priority, clearly defined skills or concepts crucial to their academic success (WWC, 2009a). Within intensive instruction, students have many opportunities to respond and receive immediate, corrective feedback with teachers and peers to practice what they are learning. Their progress is continuously monitored to determine the effectiveness of instruction, and teachers adjust instruction accordingly.

Intensive instruction is delivered by highly trained educators, typically reading specialists, special educators, or other academic or behavioral specialists. To intensify instruction, teachers use both quantitative (e.g., increasing instructional time, reducing group size) and qualitative (e.g., integrating strategies that support cognitive processes such as self-regulation and memory with academic instruction and behavior instruction, making instructional delivery more explicit and systematic and increase opportunities for feedback) adaptations (Vaughn, Wanzek, Murray, & Roberts, 2012). Teachers flexibly choose which of these features to adjust in response to student performance data.

Through the DBI framework, special education teachers closely monitor the effectiveness of a supplementary intervention. When students are not making adequate progress with research-validated supplementary interventions, special educators first intensify instruction by decreasing the group size or increasing the instructional time (Vaughn, et. al., 2012). If these quantitative changes are not sufficient, teachers can intensify instruction by modifying instructional delivery. This includes integrating qualitative strategies to support cognitive processing such as making instruction more explicit and systematic and integrating strategies to support self-regulation, memory, and self-monitoring (Vaughn, et. al., 2012). For example, special educators may model a math problem-solving strategy using think-alouds and visuals and then introduce a mnemonic to help students remember the strategy.

Research Support

Despite decades of research on special education, there is little research on instruction that is most effective for the 3 to 5% of students with the most severe learning difficulties. In addition, the efficacy of these interventions has not been adequately assessed when delivered within a tiered intervention framework. Recommendations such as those in the IES Practice Guide on intensive instruction and intervention (WWC, 2009a) are based on the opinions of an expert panel.

As noted, teachers make quantitative changes to instruction such as increasing the amount of instructional time provided or reducing the size of the group (Coyne, et al., in press; D. Fuchs, Fuchs & Vaughn, 2014; Vaughn et al., 2012). Research suggests that it takes students with disabilities at least 10 to 30 times more trials to master a skill than it does students without disabilities (WWC, 2009a). Intensity can be increased by providing longer instructional sessions or having more frequent sessions (Harn, Linan-Thompson & Roberts, 2008; Vaughn et al., 2012). One-on-one or small-group instruction allows students more opportunities to practice, respond, and receive individualized feedback (WWC, 2009a; Hattie & Timperley, 2007; Okilwa & Shelby, 2010).

Findings from research suggest that executive functioning and its underlying components have a significant effect on general academic success including reading, math, and writing (Barnett et. al., 2008; Blair, 2002; Blair & Razza, 2007; Dembo & Eaton, 2000; Diamond, Barnett, Thomas, & Munro, 2007). Executive functioning skills include working memory, mental flexibility (i.e., selective and sustained attention), and inhibitory control. Many students with intensive needs have depressed executive functioning abilities and thus struggle to plan, regulate their performance and emotions, think flexibly about a problem,

> *To intensify instruction, teachers use both quantitative and qualitative adaptations.*

and manipulate information so that it can be stored in memory. To overcome limitations in this area, students need to learn planning, problem-solving, and self-monitoring approaches in both social and academic areas. When integrated into academic and social learning, these approaches can improve students' achievement and social problem solving (Agran, Blanchard, Wehmeyer & Hughes, 2002; Boekaerts & Cascallar, 2006). Intensifying instruction by making it more explicit is beneficial to students with learning disabilities and across content areas (Baker et al., 2002; Biancarosa & Snow, 2004; Gersten et al., 2009; National Reading Panel, 2000; J. M. Smith, Saez & Doabler, 2016; H. L. Swanson, 2000; Vaughn et al., 2000).

Conclusion

Although many students make adequate progress with research-validated interventions (e.g., Tier 2 instruction), a number of students do not make progress even with these interventions and require a more intensive approach. Intensive instruction is provided within the evidence-based systematic framework of DBI (D. Fuchs et al., 2014). Over a decade of research indicates that students with disabilities who do not make sufficient progress in general education settings (Tier 1) or with supplemental interventions (Tier 2) require instruction that is more intense along a number of dimensions in order to make significant gains. Intensive instruction is highly responsive to student data and flexibly integrates these

HLP21	Teach students to maintain and generalize new learning across time and settings.

Effective teachers use specific techniques to teach students to generalize and maintain newly acquired knowledge and skills. Using numerous examples in designing and delivering instruction requires students to apply what they have learned in other settings. Educators promote maintenance by systematically using schedules of reinforcement, providing frequent material reviews, and teaching skills that are reinforced by the natural environment beyond the classroom. Students learn to use new knowledge and skills in places and situations other than the original learning environment and maintain their use in the absence of ongoing instruction.

aspects according to the individual needs of students.

Generalization and maintenance of newly acquired knowledge and skills by learners is a pervasive problem for students with disabilities, particularly those with autism spectrum disorder (Brown & Bebko, 2012; Phillips & Vollmer, 2012). *Generalization* involves performing a behavior in environments that differ from the teaching

environment (Lee & Axelrod, 2005). Haring and Eaton (1978) suggested that skill development progresses in an orderly sequence: initial accuracy (acquisition), followed by fluency and maintenance, which are followed by generalization. Effective teachers must therefore have the knowledge and skills to incorporate generalization when designing and implementing instruction. Generalization of skills must be systematically programmed instead of assuming it will automatically occur (Alberto & Troutman, 2013; Schindler & Horner, 2005). In order to generalize academic and social learning to settings other than where learning takes place, students need the opportunity to use skills in a variety of settings, with a variety of instructors. Specific instructional techniques include teaching behaviors that can be used in many different situations, teaching the behavior in several different settings with several different instructors, varying instructions and reinforcers, and programming for common stimuli between the natural and teaching settings.

Maintenance of behavior is also essential to the process of learning. *Maintenance* occurs when newly acquired skills are used in the absence of ongoing instruction. Effective teachers use schedules of reinforcement, systematic reviews of material, and other techniques to promote maintenance of behavior in novel settings thereby lessening dependence on the teacher (Lee & Axelrod, 2005). They thoughtfully and carefully choose strategies for maintenance and generalization at the onset of teaching new academic or social behaviors and build these strategies into the instructional program.

> *In order to generalize academic and social learning to settings other than where learning takes place, students need the opportunity to use skills in a variety of settings.*

Research Support

In their seminal work on generalization examining 270 articles in behavior analyses, Stokes and Baer (1977) found 120 that were related to generalization. From these, they summarized eight techniques for programming generalization: (a) sequential modification, (b) introduction of natural maintaining contingencies, (c) training sufficient exemplars, (d) training loosely, (e) using indiscriminable contingencies, (f) programming common stimuli, (g) mediating generalization, and (h) training to generalize. Since that time, studies have assessed the effectiveness of programming for maintenance and generalization on academics, social skills, and behavior in a variety of settings with a wide age range of students.

Mesmer, Duhon, and Dodson (2007), for example, used a generalization technique (i.e., programming common stimuli) to facilitate generalization of completion of academic tasks across settings with students with developmental delays and emotional disorders. Falcomata and Wacker (2013) found that generalization of the treatment effects of functional communication training for students with challenging behaviors could be enhanced through the use of specific techniques for programming generalization. Generalization techniques have been used to promote oral reading fluency (Duhon, House, Poncy, Hastings, & McClurg, 2010; Silber & Martens, 2010) and to increase maintenance of effects of a writing intervention (Hier & Eckert, 2016). Burns and colleagues (2013) suggested using Stokes and Baer's (1977) framework for programming generalization for sustaining RTI initiatives in schools. Students with autism spectrum disorder have an increased need for generalization training particularly with transferring peer interaction and social skills from small-group or resource-room settings to general education classroom and other settings. Programming specific generalization techniques has been effective in promoting social interactions (Deitchman, Reeve, Reeve, & Progar, 2010; Ducharme & Holborn, 1997; J. Jones, Lerman, & Lechago, 2014), promoting task accuracy and independence in first-grade students across settings (Hume, Plavnick, & Odom, 2012), and facilitating conversation skills (Spencer & Higbee, 2012). Freeland and Noell (1999, 2002) used intermittent reinforcement to study maintenance of students' math performance.

Conclusion

Systematically programming for generalization and maintenance of new learning has a wide range of empirical evidence to support its use as an effective practice when teaching students with disabilities to main-

tain social and academic skills and use them in a variety of settings with a variety of instructors. The techniques originally reported by Stokes and Baer (1977) have been used as interventions across a variety of studies. The vast majority of generalization and maintenance studies used single-case methodology, as it is appropriate for intervention research to improve outcomes of students with disabilities. Based on guidelines to determine whether a single-case intervention study meets criteria as an evidence-based practice (Horner et al., 2005), the studies referenced here do reflect evidence-based practice.

HLP22	**Provide positive and constructive feedback to guide students' learning and behavior.**

The purpose of feedback is to guide student learning and behavior and increase student motivation, engagement, and independence, leading to improved student learning and behavior. Effective feedback must be strategically delivered and goal directed; feedback is most effective when the learner has a goal and the feedback informs the learner regarding areas needing improvement and ways to improve performance. Feedback may be verbal, nonverbal, or written, and should be timely, contingent, genuine, meaningful, age appropriate, and at rates commensurate with task and phase of learning (i.e., acquisition, fluency, maintenance). Teachers should provide ongoing feedback until learners reach their established learning goals.

Note. As discussed in the Preface, two research syntheses were developed for the practice of providing effective feedback; this item appears in both the Social/Emotional/Behavioral Practices HLPs and the Instruction HLPs.

The purposes of instructional feedback are to guide students' learning and increase their motivation, engagement, and independence, leading to improved academic achievement. Feedback is used to elicit what students know related to academic content, and to provide direct support regarding what students need to do to learn. Feedback should be timely, meaningful, genuine, specific but succinct,

and age-appropriate, and takes many forms including questioning, scaffolding instruction, providing written comments, and providing computer-mediated feedback (Brookhart, 2008; Doabler, Nelson, & Clarke, 2016; Hattie & Timperley, 2007; Thurlings, Vermeulen, Bastiaens, & Stijnen, 2013). Feedback using programmed instruction or the use of extrinsic rewards is not highly effective in improving achievement

(Hattie, 2008). Moreover, rewards are not a central feature of effective instructional feedback, which should be designed to provide information regarding the student's performance relative to a task.

Feedback should be goal-directed; that is, it is most effective when the learner has a goal and the feedback informs the learner regarding how he or she is doing relative to the goal, and what needs to be done to improve progress (Doabler et al., 2016; Hattie, 2008). Feedback should be clear and tangible, providing the learner with an action that may be taken in response to the feedback that leads toward learning content (Thurlings et al., 2013). Teachers should also use appropriate and meaningful language, make connections to prior learning, and remind students what they already know (Doabler et al., 2016). Different forms of feedback may be provided, including feedback about whether content was correct or incorrect, discussing strategies that were used or could be used for more effective learning, and addressing students' self-regulation (e.g., whether a useful strategy is being applied to solve a problem; Hattie & Timperley, 2007). These types of feedback vary depending on the student's knowledge regarding the content. For example, providing a student with error-correction feedback when initially learning content or a skill can improve learning rate, whereas providing error correction when building fluency relative to content can negatively influence learning (Hattie & Timperley, 2007).

Feedback is most effective when addressing faulty interpretations of information (e.g., an inefficient or ineffective strategy to solve a problem), and providing cues to guide the learner toward the use of a more efficient or effective strategy or clearer understanding (Hattie, 2008; Thurlings et al., 2013). Feedback should be used to engage a student in self-evaluation, too, helping students to develop error identification skills and increase their self-regulation, independence, and confidence in learning academic content (Hattie & Timperley, 2007).

Research Support

The use of feedback to improve student learning is emphasized in standards from several professional groups, including the InTASC Standards (CCSSO, 2011), CEC's preparation standards (2016), and the National Board of Professional Teaching standards (2012). Research supports the effectiveness of feedback that is used to guide the learning of students and increase their motivation, engagement, and independence, thereby leading to improved learning. Several reviews of research have concluded that effective instructional feedback has a powerful influence on learning and achievement (Coalition for Psychology in Schools and Education, 2015; Deans for Impact, 2015; Hattie & Timperley, 2007; Thurlings et al., 2013). *Effective feedback* is (a) clear, specific, explanatory, and timely; (b) addresses a faulty interpretation of content and not a lack of understanding; and (c) emphasizes the goal of learning, the progress that is being made toward the goal, and what the student needs to do to make better progress. Further, the timing and focus of feedback are important to its effectiveness; for example, for students who are struggling and have limited understanding of content, the teacher should provide explicit instruction rather than feedback. Finally, research

> *Several reviews of research have concluded that effective instructional feedback has a powerful influence on learning and achievement.*

has shown that feedback is effective in improving achievement for students with disabilities and English language learners (WWC, 2014), including those who are struggling with reading (WWC, 2009a), writing (WWC, 2012), and mathematics (WWC, 2009b).

Conclusion

Feedback is among the most powerful influences on student achievement (Hattie,

2008). Using feedback effectively requires that teachers have substantial expertise in monitoring what the student knows about a skill or particular content area, and using this information to provide feedback that supports student learning. When feedback is used consistently and well, student educational achievement is significantly enhanced (Hattie & Timperley, 2007).

References

Adams, G. L., & Engelmann, S. (1996). *Research on direct instruction: 20 years beyond DISTAR*. Seattle, WA: Educational Achievement Systems.

Agran, M., Blanchard, C., Wehmeyer, M., & Hughes, C. (2002). Increasing the problem-solving skills of students with developmental disabilities participating in general education. *Remedial and Special Education, 23*, 279-288. doi:10.11 77/07419325020230050301

Alberto, P., & Troutman, A. (2013). *Applied behavior analysis for teachers* (9th ed.). Upper Saddle River, NJ: Pearson Education.

Al Otaiba, S., & Fuchs, D. (2002). Characteristics of children who are unresponsive to early literacy intervention: A review of the literature. *Remedial and Special Education, 23*, 300-316. doi:10.1177/07419325020230050501

Alper, S., & Raharinirina, S. (2006). Assistive technology for individuals with disabilities: A review and synthesis of the literature. *Journal of Special Education Technology, 21*, 47-64.

Appleton, J. J., Christenson, S. L., & Furlong, M. J. (2008). Student engagement with school: Critical conceptual and methodological issues of the construct. *Psychology in the Schools. 45*, 369-386. doi:10.1002/pits.20303

Archambault, I., Janosz, M., Morizot, J., & Pagani, L. (2009). Adolescent behavioral, affective, and cognitive engagement in school: Relationship to dropout. *Journal of School Health, 79*, 408-415. doi:10.1111/j.1746-1561.2009.00428.x

Archer, A. L., & Hughes, C. A. (2011). *Explicit instruction: Effective and efficient teaching*. New York, NY: Guilford.

Baker, S., Gersten, R., & Lee, D. (2002). A synthesis of empirical research on teaching mathematics to low-achieving students. *The Elementary School Journal, 103*, 51-73. doi:10.1086/499715

Baker, S. K., Chard, D., Ketterlin-Geller, L. R., Apichatabutra, C., & Doabler, C. (2009). Teaching writing to at-risk students: The quality of evidence for self-regulated strategy development. *Exceptional Children, 75*, 303-318.

Barnett, W. S., Jung, K., Yarosz, D. J., Thomas, J., Hornbeck, A., Stechuk, R., & Burns, S. (2008). Educational effects of the Tools of the Mind curriculum: A randomized trial. *Early Childhood Research Quarterly, 23*, 299-313. doi:10.1016/j. ecresq.2008.03.001

Basham, J. D., & Marino, M. T. (2013). Understanding STEM education and supporting students through universal design for learning. *TEACHING Exceptional Children, 45*(4), 8-15. doi:10.1177/004005991304500401

Best Evidence Encyclopedia. (n.d.). *Direct instruction/corrective reading*. Retrieved from www.bestevidence.org/overviews/D/di.htm

Biancarosa, G., & Snow, C. E. (2004). *Reading next–A vision for action and research in middle and high school literacy: A report to Carnegie Corporation of New York* (2nd ed.). Washington, DC: Alliance for Excellence in Education. https://www.carnegie.org/media/filer_public/b7/5f/b75fba81-16cb-422d-ab59-373a6a07eb74/ccny_report_2004_reading.pdf

Billingsley, B., Brownell, M., Israel, M., & Kaaman, M. (2013). *A survival guide for new special educators*. San Francisco, CA: Jossey-Bass Teacher.

Blair, C. (2002). School readiness: Integrating cognition and emotion in a neurobiological conceptualization of children's functioning at school entry. *American Psychologist, 57*, 111–127. doi:10.1037//0003-066X.57.2.111

Blair, C., & Razza, R. P. (2007). Relating effortful control, executive function, and false belief understanding to emerging math and literacy ability in kindergarten. *Child Development, 78*, 647–663. doi:10.1111/j.1467-8624.2007.01019.x

Boardman, A. G., Swanson, E., Klingner, J. K., & Vaughn, S. (2013). Using collaborative strategic reading to improve reading comprehension. In B. B. Cook & Tankersley (Eds.), *Research-based practices in special education* (pp. 33–46). Upper Saddle River, NJ: Pearson

Boekaerts, M., & Cascallar, E. (2006). How far have we moved toward the integration of theory and practice in self-regulation? *Educational Psychology Review, 18*, 199–210. doi:10.1007/s10648-006-9013-4

Bottge, B. A., Toland, M. D., Gassaway, L., Butler, M., Choo, S., Griffen, A. K., & Ma, X. (2015). Impact of enhanced anchored instruction in inclusive math classrooms. *Exceptional Children, 81*, 158–175.

Brigham, R., & Brigham, M. (2001, Summer). Mnemonic instruction. *Current Practice Alerts, 5*. Retrieved from http://s3.amazonaws.com/cmi-teaching-ld/alerts/14/uploaded_files/original_Alert5.pdf?1301001560

Brookhart, S. M. (2008). *How to give effective feedback to your students*. Alexandria, VA: ASCD.

Brophy, J. E. (1986). Teacher influences on student achievement. *American Psychologist, 4*, 1069–1077. doi:10.1037/0003-066X.41.10.1069

Brophy, J. E., & Good, T. L. (1986). Teacher behavior and student achievement. In M. C. Wittrock (Ed.), *Handbook of research on teaching* (3rd ed., pp. 328–375). New York, NY: Macmillan

Browder, D. M., Spooner, F., Ahlgrim-Delzell, L., Flowers, C., Algozzine, B., & Karvonen, M. (2003). A Content analysis of the curricular philosophies reflected in states' alternate assessment performance indicators. *Research and Practice for Persons with Severe Disabilities, 28*, 165–181. doi:10.2511/rpsd.28.4.165

Brown, S. M., & Bebko, J. M. (2012). Generalization, overselectivity, and discrimination in the autism phenotype: A review. *Research in Autism Spectrum Disorders, 6*, 733–740. doi:10.1016/j.rasd.2011.10.012

Bruhn, A., McDaniel, S., & Kreigh, C. (2015). Self-monitoring interventions for students with behavior problems: A systematic review of current research. *Behavioral Disorders, 40*, 102–121. doi:10.17988/BD-13-45.1

Bulgren, J. A. (2006). Integrated content enhancement routines: Responding to the needs of adolescents with disabilities in rigorous inclusive secondary content classes. *TEACHING Exceptional Children, 38*(6), 54–58. doi:10.1177/004005990603800608

Burns, M. K., Egan, A. M., Kunkel, A. K., McComas, J., Peterson, M. M., Rahn, N. L. & Wilson, J. (2013). Training for generalization and maintenance in RtI implementation: Front-loading for sustainability. *Learning Disabilities Research & Practice, 28*, 81–88. doi:10.1111/ldrp.12009

CAST. (2016, February 17). *UDL in the ESSA*. Retrieved from http://www.cast.org/whats-new/news/2016/udl-in-the-essa.html#.WGQTUlMrKUk

Chard, D. (n.d.). Differentiating instruction for students with special needs. *Houghton-Mifflin Harcourt Journeys*. Retrieved from http://www.doe.in.gov/sites/default/files/curriculum/chard-special-education-paper.pdf

Charles, R.I., (2005). Big ideas and understandings as the foundation for elementary and middle school mathematics. *Journal of Mathematics Education Leadership, 7*(3), 9–24.

Christenson, S.L., Sinclair, M.F., Lehr, C.A., & Godber, Y. (2001). Promoting successful school completion: Critical conceptual and methodological guidelines. *School Psychology Quarterly, 16*, 468–484. doi:10.1521/scpq.16.4.468.19898

Christenson, S.L., & Thurlow, M.L. (2004). School dropouts: Prevention considerations, interventions, and challenges. *Current Directions in Psychological Science, 13*(1), 36–39. doi:10.1111/j.0963-7214.2004.01301010.x

Coalition for Psychology in Schools and Education. (2015). *Top 20 principles from psychology for preK–12 teaching and learning*. Washington, DC: American Psychological Association. Retrieved from http:// www.apa.org/ed/schools/cpse/top-twenty-principles.pdf

Cohen, E. G., & Lotan, R. A. (2014). *Designing group work: Strategies for the heterogeneous classroom* (3rd. ed.). New York, NY: Teachers College.

Collins, B., Hager, K. L., & Galloway, C. C. (2011). Addition of functional content during core content instruction for students with moderate disabilities. *Education and Training in Autism and Developmental Disabilities, 46*, 22–19.

Common Core State Standards Initiative. (n.d.). *Application to students with disabilities*. Retrieved from http://www.corestandards.org/wp-content/uploads/Application-to-Students-with-Disabilities-again-for-merge1.pdf

Connor, C., Jakobsons, L., Crowe, E., & Meadows, J. (2009). Instruction, student engagement, and reading skill growth in Reading First classrooms. *The Elementary School Journal, 109*, 221–250. doi:10.1086/592305

Connor, C. M., Piasta, S. B., Fishman, B., Glasney, S., Schatschneider, C., Crowe, E., … Morrison, F. J. (2009). Individualizing student instruction precisely: Effects of child × instruction interactions on first graders' literacy development. *Child Development, 80*, 77–100. doi:10.1111/j.1467-8624.2008.01247.x

Consortium for Policy Research in Education. (2011, January). *Learning trajectories in mathematics: A foundation for standards, curriculum, assessment and instruction* (CPRE Research Report # RR-68). Philadelphia, PA: Author. Retrieved from http://www.cpre.org/sites/default/files/researchreport/1220_learningtrajectoriesinmathcciireport.pdf

Cook, B. G., & Cook, S. C. (2013). Unraveling evidence-based practices in special education. *The Journal of Special Education, 47*, 71–82. doi:10.1177/0022466911420877

Cornelius-White, J. & Harbaugh, A. (2010). *Learner-centered instruction: Building relationships for student success*. Los Angeles, CA: SAGE.

Council for Exceptional Children. (2016). Preparation standards. In *What every special educator must know: Professional ethics and standards* (pp. 19–34). Arlington, VA: Author.

Council of Chief State School Officers. (2011, April). *InTASC model core teaching standards: A resource for state dialogue*. Washington, DC: Author. Retrieved from www.ccsso.org/documents/2011/intasc_model_core_teaching_standards_2011.pdf

Coyne, M. D., Kame'enui, E. J., & Simmons, D. C. (2001). Improving beginning reading instruction and intervention for students with LD: Reconciling "all" with "each." *Journal of Learning Disabilities, 37*, 231–239. doi:10.1177/00222194040370030801

Coyne, M. D., Simmons, D. C., Hagan-Burke, S., Simmons, L. E., Kwok, O., Kim, M., Fogarty, M., … Rawlinson, D. M. (in press). Adjusting beginning reading intervention based on student performance: An experimental evaluation. *Exceptional Children*.

Coyne, M. D., Simmons, D. C., Kame'enui, E. J., & Stoolmiller, M. (2004). Teaching vocabulary during shared storybook readings: An examination of differential effects. *Exceptionality, 12*, 145–162. doi:10.1207/s15327035ex1203_3

Deans for Impact. (2015). *The science of learning*. Retrieved from www.deansforimpact.org/the_science_of_learning.html

Deitchman, C., Reeve, S. A., Reeve, K. F., & Progar, P. R. (2010). Incorporating video feedback into self-management training to promote generalization of social initiations by children with autism. *Education and Treatment of Children, 33*, 475–488. doi:10.1353/etc.0.0102

Dembo, M. H., & Eaton, M. J. (2000). Self-regulation of academic learning in middle level schools. *Elementary School Journal, 100*, 473–490. doi:10.1086/499651

Deshler, D. D., Schumaker, J. B., Bulgren, J. A., Lenz, B. K., Jantzen, J., Adams, G., … Marquis, J. (2001). Making things easier: Connecting knowledge to things students already know. *TEACHING Exceptional Children, 33*(4), 82–85. doi:10.1177/004005990103300412

Dexter, D., & Hughes, C. A. (2011). Graphic organizers and students with learning disabilities: a meta-analysis. *Learning Disabilities Quarterly, 34*, 51–72. doi:10.1177/073194871103400104

Diamond, A., Barnett, W. S., Thomas, J., & Munro, S. (2007). Preschool program improves cognitive control. *Science, 318*, 1387–1388. doi:10.1126/science.1151148

Doabler, C. T., Cary, M. S., Junghohann, K., Clarke, B., Fien, H., Baker, S., … Chard, D. (2012). Enhancing core mathematics instruction for students at risk for mathematics disabilities. *TEACHING Exceptional Children, 44*(4), 48–57. doi:10.1177/004005991204400405

Doabler, C. T., Nelson, N. J., & Clarke, B. (2016). Adapting evidence-based practices to meet the needs of English learners with mathematics difficulties. *TEACHING Exceptional Children, 48*, 301–310. doi:10.1177/0040059916650638

Ducharme, D. E., & Holborn, S. W. (1997). Programming generalization of social skills in preschool children with hearing impairments. *Journal of Applied Behavior Analysis, 30*, 639–651. doi:10.1901/jaba.1997.30-639

Duhon, G. J., House, S. E., Poncy, B. C., Hastings, K. W., & McClurg, S. C. (2010). An examination of two techniques for promoting response generalization of early literacy skills. *Journal of Behavioral Education, 19*, 62–75. doi:10.1007/s10864-010-9097-2

Dunn, C., Chambers, D., & Rabren, K. (2004). Variables affecting students' decisions to drop out of school. *Remedial and Special Education, 25*, 314–323. doi:10.1177/07419325040250050501

Dwyer, T., Blizzard, L., & Dean, K. (1996). Physical activity and performance in children. *Nutrition Review, 54*(4), 27-31. doi:10.1111/j.1753-4887.1996. tb03895.x

Dwyer, T., Sallis, J. F., Blizzard, L., Lazarus, R., & Dean, K. (2001). Relation of academic performance to physical activity and fitness in children. *Pediatric Exercise Science, 13*, 225-237. doi:10.1123/pes.13.3.225

Dye, G. A. (2000). Graphic organizers to the rescue! Helping student link—and remember—information. *TEACHING Exceptional Children, 32*(3), 72-76. doi:10.1177/004005990003200311

Edyburn, D. L. (2013). Critical issues in advancing the special education technology evidence base. *Exceptional Children, 80*, 7-24.

Ellis, E. (1991). *SLANT: A starter strategy for class participation*. Lawrence, KS: Edge Enterprises.

Ellis, E., & Howard, P. W. (2007, Spring). Graphic organizers: Power tools for teaching students with learning disabilities. *Current Practice Alerts, 13*. Retrieved from http://s3.amazonaws.com/cmi-teaching-ld/alerts/6/uploaded_files/original_alert13.pdf?1301000665

Ellis, E. S., & Worthington, L. A. (1994). *Research synthesis on effective teaching principles and the design of quality tools for educators* (Technical Report No. 5). Eugene, OR: University of Oregon, National Center to Improve the Tools of Educators.

Emmer, E. T., & Gerwels, M. (2006). Classroom management in middle and high school classrooms. In C. M. Evertson & C. S. Weinstein (Eds.), *Handbook of classroom management: Research, practice, and contemporary issues* (pp. 407-437). Mahwah, NJ: Erlbaum.

Englert, C. S., & Dunsmore, K. (2002). A diversity of teaching and learning paths: Teaching writing in situated activity. In J. Brophy (Ed.), *Social constructivist teaching: Affordances and constraints* (Vol. 9, pp. 81-130). Amsterdam, Netherlands: JAI Press.

Englert, C. S., & Mariage, T. V. (1991). Making students partners in the comprehension process: Organizing the reading "POSSE." *Learning Disability Quarterly, 14*, 123-138. doi:10.2307/1510519

Englert, C. S., Tarrant, L. K., Mariage, T. V., Oxer, T. (1994). Lesson talk as the work of reading groups: The effectiveness of two interventions. *Journal of Learning Disabilities, 27*, 165-185. doi:10.1177/002221949402700305

Erlbaum, B., Vaughn, S., Hughes, M., & Moody, S. (2000). How effective are one-to-one tutoring programs in reading for elementary students at risk for academic failure? A meta-analysis of intervention research. *Journal of Educational Psychology, 92*, 605-619. doi:10.1037/0022-0663.92.4.605

Every Student Succeeds Act, 20 U.S.C. 6301 *et seq.* (2015).

Falcomata, T. S., & Wacker, D. P. (2013). On the use of strategies for programming generalization during functional communication training: A review of the literature. *Journal of Developmental and Physical Disabilities, 25*, 5-15. doi:10.1007/s10882-012-9311-3

Finn, J. D. (1993, August). *School engagement & students at risk.* Washington, DC: National Center for Education Statistics, U.S. Department of Education. Retrieved from http://nces.ed.gov/pubs93/93470a.pdf

Finn, J. D., & Cox, D. (1992). Participation and withdrawal among fourth grade pupils. *American Educational Research Journal, 29*, 141-162. doi:10.3102/00028312029001141

Fontana, J. L., Scruggs, T., & Mastropieri, M. A. (2007). Mnemonic strategy instruction in inclusive secondary social studies classes. *Remedial and Special Education, 28*, 345-355. doi:10.1177/07419325070280060401

Forness, S. R., Kavale, K. A., Blum, I. M., & Lloyd, J. W. (1997). Mega-analysis of meta analysis. *TEACHING Exceptional Children, 29*(6), 4-9.

Freeland, J. T., & Noell, G. H. (1999). Maintaining accurate math responses in elementary school students: The effects of delayed intermittent reinforcement and programming common stimuli. *Journal of Applied Behavior Analysis, 32*, 211-215. doi:10.1901/jaba.1999.32-211

Freeland, J. T., & Noell, G. H. (2002). Programming for maintenance: An investigation of delayed intermittent reinforcement and common stimuli to create indiscriminable contingencies. *Journal of Behavioral Education, 11*, 5-18. doi:10.1023/A:1014329104102

Fuchs, D., Fuchs, L. S., & Vaughn, S. (2014). What is intensive instruction and why is it important? *TEACHING Exceptional Children, 46*(4), 13-18. doi:10.1177/0040059914522966

Fuchs, L. S., & Fuchs, D. (1986). Effects of systematic formative evaluation: A meta-analysis. *Exceptional Children, 53*, 199-208. doi:10.1177/001440298605300301

Fuchs, L. S., Fuchs, D., Compton, D.L., Wehby, J., Schumacher, R. F., Gersten, R., & Jordan, N. C. (2015). Inclusion versus specialized intervention for very low-performing students: What does access mean in an era of academic challenge? *Exceptional Children, 81*, 134-157. doi:10.1177/0014402914551743

Fuchs, L. S., Fuchs, D., Craddock, C., Hollenbeck, K. N., Hamlett, C. L., & Schatschneider, C. (2008). Effects of small group tutoring with and without validated classroom instruction on at-risk students' math problem solving: Are two tiers of prevention better than one? *Journal of Educational Psychology, 100*, 491-509. doi:10.1037/0022-0663.100.3.491

Furlong, M. J., Morrison, G. M., & Dear, J. D. (1994). Addressing school violence as part of schools' educational mission. *Preventing School Failure, 38*, 10-17. doi: 10.1080/1045988X.1994.9944308

Gajria, M., Jitendra, A. K., Sood, S., & Sacks, G. (2007). Improving comprehension of expository text in students with LD: A research synthesis. *Journal of Learning Disabilities, 40*, 210-225. doi:10.1177/00222194070400030301

Ganz, J. B., Earles-Vollrath, T. L., Heath, A. K., Parker, R. I., Rispoli, M. J., & Duran, J. B. (2012). A meta-analysis of single case research studies on aided augmented and alternative communication systems with individuals with autism spectrum disorders. *Journal of Autism and Developmental Disorders, 42*, 60-74. doi:10.1007/s10803-011-1212-2

Gersten, R., Chard, D., Jayanthi, M., Baker, S., Morphy, P., & Flojo, J. (2009). Mathematics instruction for students with learning disabilities: A meta-analysis of instructional components. *Review of Educational Research, 79*, 1202-1242. doi:10.3102/0034654309334431

Gersten, R., Schiller, E. P., & Vaughn, S. (Eds.). (2000). *Contemporary special education research: Synthesis of the knowledge base on critical instructional issues.* Mahwah, NJ: Erlbaum.

Gillespie, A., & Graham, S. (2014). A meta-analysis of writing interventions for students with learning disabilities. *Exceptional Children, 80*, 454-473. doi:10.1177/0014402914527238

Good, T., Grouws, D., & Ebmeier, M. (1983). *Active mathematics teaching.* New York, NY: Longman.

Graham, S., Harris, K. R., & Mason, L. (2005). Improving the writing performance, knowledge, and self-efficacy of struggling young writers: The effects of self-regulated strategy development. *Contemporary Educational Psychology, 30*, 207-241. doi:10.1016/j.cedpsych.2004.08.001

Graham, S., & Perin, D. (2007). A meta-analysis of writing instruction for adolescent students. *Journal of Educational Psychology, 99*, 445-476. doi:10.1037/0022-0663.99.3.445

Hamilton, S. L., Seibert, M. A., Gardner, R., III, & Talbert-Johnson, C. (2000). Using guided notes to improve the academic achievement of incarcerated adolescents with learning and behavior problems. *Remedial and Special Education, 21*, 133-140. doi:10.1177/074193250002100302

Hamre, B. K., & Pianta, R. C. (2006). Student–teacher relationships as a source of support and risk in schools. In G. G. Bear & K. M. Minke (Eds.), *Children's needs III: Development, prevention, and intervention* (pp. 59-71). Washington, DC: National Association of School Psychologists.

Hanselman, E. (2013, April). *Guidance on documenting Common Core State Standards on the individualized education program* [Letter to Directors of Special Education, District Superintendents, Other Interested Parties]. Springfield, IL: Illinois State Boards of Education. Retrieved from http://www.isbe.net/spec-ed/pdfs/guidance-ccss.pdf

Haring, N. G., & Eaton, M. D. (1978). Systematic instructional procedures: An instructional hierarchy. In N. G. Haring, T. C. Lovitt, M. D. Eaton, & C. L. Hansen (Eds.), *The fourth R: Research in the Classroom* (pp. 23-40). Columbus, OH: Merrill.

Harn, B. A., Linan-Thompson, S., & Roberts, G. (2008). Intensifying instruction. *Journal of Learning Disabilities, 41*, 115-125. doi:10.1177/0022219407313586

Harris, K. R., & Graham, S. (1996). *Making the writing process work: Strategies for composition and self-regulation.* Cambridge, MA: Brookline.

Harris, K. R., & Graham, S. (2003). Students with learning disabilities and the process of writing: A meta-analysis of SRSD studies. In H. L. Swanson, K. R. Harris, & S. Graham (Eds.), *Handbook of learning disabilities* (pp.323-344). New York, NY: Guilford.

Harris, K. R., Graham, S., & Mason, L. H. (2003). Self-regulated strategy development in the classroom: Part of a balanced approach to writing instruction for students with disabilities. *Focus on Exceptional Children, 35*(7), 1-16. Retrieved from https://srsdonline.org/wp-content/uploads/2015/12/Harris-Graham-Mason-2003.pdf

Hattie, J. (2008). *Visible learning: A synthesis of over 800 meta-analyses relating to achievement.* London, England: Routledge.

Hattie, J., & Timperley, H. (2007). The power of feedback. *Review of Educational Research, 77*, 81-112.

Heritage, M. (2009). *Learning progressions: Supporting instruction and formative assessment.* Washington, DC: Formative Assessment for Students and Teachers State Collaborative on Assessment and Student Standards, Council of Chief State School Officers. Retrieved from http://www.k12.wa.us/assessment/ClassroomAssessmentIntegration/pubdocs/FASTLearningProgressions.pdf

Hemmeter, M. L., Santos, R. M., & Ostrosky, M. M. (2008). Preparing early childhood educators to address young children's social emotional development and challenging behavior. *Journal of Early Intervention, 30*, 321-340. doi:10.1177/1053815108320900

Hess, K. K. (2011, December). *Learning progressions frameworks designed for use with the Common Core State Standards in English Language Arts & Literacy K-12.* Retrieved from http://www.naacpartners.org/publications/ELA_LPF_12.2011_final.pdf

Heward, W. L. (1994). Three "low tech" strategies for increasing the frequency of active student response during group instruction. In R. Gardner, D. M. Sainato, J. O. Cooper, T. E. Heron, W. L., Heward, J. Eshleman, & T. A. Grossi (Eds.), *Behavior analysis in education: Focus on measurably effective instruction* (pp. 283–320). Monterey, CA: Cole/Brooks.

Heward, W. L., & Wood, C. L. (2015, April). *Improving educational outcomes in America: Can a low tech, generic teaching practice make a difference?* Oakland, CA: Wing Institute for Evidence Based Practice.

Hier, B. O., & Eckert, T. L. (2016). Programming generality into a performance feedback writing intervention: A randomized controlled trial. *Journal of School Psychology, 56*, 111–131. doi:10.1016/j.jsp.2016.03.003

Hoffman, J., (2002). Flexible grouping strategies in the multiage classroom. *Theory into Practice, 41*(1), 47–52. doi:10.1207/s15430421tip4101_8

Horner, R. H., Carr, E. G., Halle, J., McGee, G., Odom, S., & Woolery, M. (2005). The use of single-subject research to identify evidence-based practice in special education. *Exceptional Children, 71*, 165–179. doi:10.1177/001440290507100203

Horton, P. B., McConney, A. A., Gallo, M., Woods, A. L., Senn, G. J., & Hamelin, D. (1993). An investigation of the effectiveness of concept mapping as an instructional tool. *Science Education, 77*(1), 95–111. doi:10.1002/sce.3730770107

Hughes, C. A. (2011). Effective design and delivery of task-specific learning strategy instruction for students with learning disabilities. *Focus on Exceptional Children, 44*(2), 1–16. Retrieved from http://s101.podbean.com/pb/4da83704eb775f83b117d5ac553977fd/5863dfca/data2/fs32/609421/uploads/70235641.pdf

Hume, K., Plavnick, J., & Odom, S. L. (2012). Promoting task accuracy and independence in students with autism across educational setting through the use of individual work systems. *Journal of Autism and Developmental Disorders, 42*, 2084–2099. doi:10.1007/s10803-012-1457-4

IDEA regulations, 34 C.F.R. § 300 (2012).

Individuals With Disabilities Education Act, 20 U.S.C. §§ 1400 *et seq.* (2006 & Supp. V. 2011)

International Literacy Association. (2010). *Standards 2010: Pre-K and elementary classroom teacher.* Retrieved from https://www.literacyworldwide.org/get-resources/standards/standards-for-reading-professionals/standards-2010-role-2

Israel, M., Marino, M., Desilio, L., & Serianni, B. (2014, September). Supporting content learning through technology for K-12 students with disabilities (CEEDAR Document No. IC-10). Retrieved from http://ceedar.education.ufl.edu/wp-content/uploads/2014/09/IC-10_FINAL_09-10-14.pdf

Iverson, S., Tunmer, W., & Chapman, J. (2005). The effects of varying group size on the reading recovery approach to preventive early intervention. *Journal of Learning Disabilities, 38*, 456-472. doi:10.1177/00222194050380050801

Ives, B. (2007). Graphic organizers applied to secondary algebra instruction for students with learning disabilities. *Learning Disabilities Research & Practice, 22*, 110-118. 10.1111/j.1540-5826.2007.00235.x

Jackson, D. (2015). *A retrospective study of student engagement among at-risk elementary students with and without disabilities* (Doctoral dissertation). Retrieved from http://pqdtopen.proquest.com/doc/1671779397.html?FMT=AI

Jensen, E. (2013). *Engaging students with poverty in mind: Practical strategies for raising achievement.* Alexandria, VA: ASCD.

Jitendra, A. K. (2007). *Solving math word problems: Teaching students with learning disabilities using schema-based instruction.* Austin, TX: PRO-ED.

Jitendra, A. K., Burgess, C., & Gajria, M. (2011). Cognitive strategy instruction for improving expository text comprehension of students with learning disabilities: The quality of evidence. *Exceptional Children, 77*, 135-159. doi:10.1177/001440291107700201

Jitendra, A. K., & Star, J. R. (2011). Meeting the needs of students with learning disabilities in inclusive mathematics classrooms: The role of schema-based instruction on mathematical problem-solving. *Theory Into Practice, 50*, 12-19. doi:10.1080/00405841.2011.534912

Johnson, D. W., & Johnson, R. T. (1987). Research shows the benefits of adult cooperation. *Educational Leadership, 45*(3), 27-30.

Johnson, D. W., & Johnson, R. T. (2002). Learning together and alone: Overview and meta analysis. *Asia Pacific Journal of Education, 53*(1), 95-105. doi:10.1080/0218879020220110

Johnson, D. W., Johnson, R. T. & Maruyama, G. (1983). Interdependence and interpersonal attraction among heterogeneous and homogeneous individuals: A theoretical formulation and a meta-analysis of the research. *Review of Educational Research, 53*, 5-54. doi:10.3102/00346543053001005

Johnson, D. W., Maruyama, G., Johnson, R. T., Nelson, D., & Skon, L. (1981). Effects of cooperative, competitive, and individualistic goal structures on achievement: A meta-analysis. *Psychological Bulletin, 89*(1), 47-62. doi:10.1037/0033-2909.89.1.47

Jones, C. B., Reutzel, D. R., & Smith, J. A. (2012). A focus on struggling readers: A comparative analysis of expert opinion and empirical research recommendations. In R. F. Flippo (Ed.), *Reading researchers in search of common ground: The expert study revisited* (pp. 274-304). Abingdon-on-Thames, England: Routledge.

Jones, J., Lerman, D. C., & Lechago, S. (2014). Assessing stimulus control and promoting generalization via video modeling when teaching social responses to children with autism. *Journal of Applied Behavior Analysis, 47*, 37–50. doi:10.1002/jaba.81

Kagan, S., & Kagan, M. (2009). *Kagan cooperative learning*. San Clemente, CA: Kagan Publishing.

Kaldenberg, E. R., Watt, S. J., & Therrien, W. J. (2015). Reading instruction in science for students with learning disabilities: A meta-analysis. *Learning Disability Quarterly, 38*, 160–173. doi:10.1177/0731948714550204

Karl, J., Collins, B. C., Hager, K. D., & Ault, M. J. (2013). Teaching core content embedded in a functional activity to students with moderate intellectual disability using a simultaneous prompting procedure. *Education and Training in Autism and Developmental Disabilities, 48*, 363–378.

Kennedy, C. H. (2005). *Single-case designs for educational research*. Boston, MA: Pearson/Allyn & Bacon.

Kennedy, M. J., & Deshler, D. D. (2010). Literacy instruction, technology, and students with learning disabilities: Research we have, research we need. *Learning Disability Quarterly, 33*, 289–298. doi:10.1177/073194871003300406

Kim, A. H., Vaughn, S., Wanzek, J., & Wei, S. (2004). Graphic organizers and their effects on the reading comprehension of students with LD: A synthesis of research. *Journal of Learning Disabilities, 37*, 105–118. doi:10.1177/00222194 040370020201

Klein, H. J., Wesson, M. J., Hollenbeck, J. R., & Alge, B. J. (1999). Goal commitment and the goal-setting process: Conceptual clarification and empirical synthesis. *Journal of Applied Psychology, 84*, 885–896. doi:10.1037/0021-9010.84.6.885

Kleinheksel, K. A., & Summy, S. E. (2003). Enhancing student learning and social behavior through mnemonic strategies. *TEACHING Exceptional Children, 36*(2), 30–35. doi:10.1177/004005990303600204

Klem, A. M., & Connell, J. P. (2009). Relationships matter: Linking teacher support to student engagement and achievement. *Journal of School Health, 74*, 262–273. doi:10.1111/j.1746-1561.2004.tb08283.x

Klingner, J. K., & Vaughn, S. (1996). Reciprocal teaching of reading comprehension strategies for students with learning disabilities who are English language learners. *Elementary School Journal, 96*, 275–29. doi:10.1086/461828

Klingner, J. K., Vaughn, S., Dimino, J., Schumm, J. S., & Bryant, D. (2001). *From clunk to click: Collaborative strategic reading*. Longmont, CO: Sopris West.

Konrad, M., Joseph, L. M., & Eveleigh, E. (2009). A meta-analytic review of guided notes. *Education and Treatment of Children, 32*, 421–444. doi:10.1353/etc.0.0066

Krawec, J., Huang, J., Montague, M., Kressler, B., & de Alba, A. M. (2013). The effects of cognitive strategy instruction on knowledge of math problem-solving processes of middle-school students with disabilities. *Learning Disability Quarterly, 36*, 80–92. doi:10.1177/0731948712463368

Kubesch S., Walk, L., Spitzer, M., Kammer, T., Laiburg, A., Heim, R., & Hille, K. (2009). A 30-minute physical education program improves students' executive attention. *Mind, Brain, and Education, 3*, 235–242. doi:10.1111/j.1751-228X.2009.01076.x

Lederer, J. M. (2000). Reciprocal teaching of social studies in inclusive elementary classes. *Journal of Learning Disabilities, 33*, 91–106. doi:10.1177/002221940003300112

Lee, D. L., & Axelrod, S. A. (2005). *Behavior modification: Basic principles* (3rd ed.). Austin, TX: PRO-ED.

Lenz, B. K., & Bulgren, J. (2013). Improving academic outcomes in the content areas. In B. B. Cook & M. G. Tankersley (Eds.), *Research-based practices in special education* (pp. 98–115). Upper Saddle River, NJ: Pearson.

Marchand-Martella, N. E., Slocum, T. A., & Martella, R. C. (Eds.). (2004). *Introduction to direct instruction*. Boston, MA: Pearson Education.

Marzano, R., & Pickering, D. (2011). *The highly engaged classroom*. Bloomington, IN: Marzano Research Laboratory.

Mason, L. H., Harris, K. R., & Graham, S. (2011). Self-regulated strategy development for students with writing difficulties. *Theory Into Practice, 50*, 20–27. doi:10.10 80/00405841.2011.534922

Mastropieri, M. A., & Scruggs, T. E. (2010). *The inclusive classroom: Strategies for effective instruction* (4th ed.). Upper Saddle River, NJ: Pearson

Mastropieri, M. A., Scruggs, T. E., & Levin, J. R. (1985). Maximizing what exceptional children can learn: A review of research on the keyword method and related mnemonic techniques. *Remedial and Special Education, 6*, 39–45. doi:10.1177/074193258500600208

Mayer, R. E. (2008). Applying the science of learning: Evidence-based principles for the design of multimedia instruction. *American Psychologist, 63*, 760–769. doi:10.1037/0003-066X.63.8.760

McLeskey, J., Landers, E., Williamson, P., & Hoppey, D. (2012). The least restrictive environment mandate of IDEA: Are we moving toward educating students with disabilities in less restrictive settings? *The Journal of Special Education, 36*, 131–140. doi:10.1177/0022466910376670

McLeskey, J., & Waldron, N. L. (2011). Educational programs for elementary students with learning disabilities: Can they be both effective and inclusive? *Learning Disabilities Research & Practice, 26*, 48-57. doi:10.1111/j.1540-5826.2010.00324.x

McMaster, K., Fuchs, D., Fuchs, L. S., & Compton, D. L. (2005). Responding to non-responders: An experimental field trial of identification and intervention methods. *Exceptional Children, 71*, 445-463. doi:10.1177/001440290507100404

Mercer, C. D., Mercer, A. R., & Pullen, P. C. (2011). *Teaching students with learning problems* (8th ed.). Boston, MA: Pearson Education.

Mesmer, E. M., Duhon, G. J., & Dodson, K. (2007). The effects of programming common stimuli for enhancing stimulus generalization of academic behavior. *Journal of Applied Behavior Analysis, 40*, 553-557. doi:10.1901/jaba.2007.40-553

Moats, L. (2014, April 3). When older kids can't read: What does the newest research say? [Webinar]. Retrieved from https://voyagersopris.wistia.com/medias/2gabrx8srf

Moats, L. C. (2000). *Speech to print: Language essentials for teachers.* Baltimore, MD: Brookes.

Montague, M., & Dietz, S. (2009). Evaluating the evidence base for cognitive strategy instruction and mathematical problem solving. *Exceptional Children, 75*, 285-302. doi:10.1177/001440290907500302

Moody, S. W., Vaughn, S., & Schumm, J. S. (1997). Instructional grouping for reading: Teachers' views. *Remedial and Special Education, 18*, 347-356. doi:10.1177/074193259701800604

Moore, D. W., & Readence, J. E. (1984). A quantitative and qualitative review of graphic organizer research. Journal of Educational Research, 78(1), 11-17.

Musti-Rao, S., Kroeger, S. D., & Schumaker-Dyke, K. (2008). Using guided notes and response cards at the postsecondary level. *Teacher Education and Special Education, 31*, 149-163. doi:10.1177/0888406408330630

National Board for Professional Teaching Standards. (2012). *Early childhood generalist standards* (3rd ed.). Arlington, VA: NBPTS. Retrieved from http://www.nbpts.org/sites/default/files/documents/certificates/nbpts-certificate-ec-gen-standards.pdf

National Board for Professional Teaching Standards. (2016). *What teachers should know and be able to do.* Arlington, VA: Author. Retrieved from http://www.nbpts.org/sites/default/files/what_teachers_should_know.pdf

National Center on Intensive Intervention. (2013, March). *Data-based individualization: A framework for intensive intervention.* Washington, DC: American Institutes for Research. Retrieved from http://www.intensiveintervention.org/sites/default/files/DBI_Framework.pdf

National Reading Panel (2000). *Teaching children to read: An evidence-based assessment of the scientific research literature on reading and its implications for reading instruction* (NIH Publication No. 00-4769). Washington DC: U.S. Department of Health and Human Services. Retrieved from https://www.nichd.nih.gov/publications/pubs/nrp/Pages/smallbook.aspx

National Technical Assistance Center on Transition. (2016, October). *Effective practices and predictors matrix.* Retrieved from http://transitionta.org/system/files/effectivepractices/Effective%20Practices%20and%20Predictors%20Matrix%2012-21-16.pdf?file=1&type=node&id=1124&force

Nesbit, J. C., & Adesope, O. O. (2006). Learning with concepts and knowledge maps: A meta analysis. *Review of Educational Research, 76,* 413-448. doi:10.3102/00346543076003413

Newell, A. (1990). *Unified theories of cognition.* Cambridge, MA: Harvard University Press.

Office of the Superintendent of Public Instruction & Washington Education Association. (n.d.). *Common Core instruction and special education* [Presentation PDF]. Retrieved from: http://www.k12.wa.us/SpecialEd/ResourceLibrary/default.aspx

Okilwa, N. S. A., & Shelby, L. (2010). The effects of peer tutoring on academic performance of students with disabilities in grades 6 through 12: A synthesis of the literature. *Remedial and Special Education, 31,* 450-463. doi:10.1177/0741932509355991

Okolo, C. M., & Bahr, C. M. (1995). Increasing achievement motivation of elementary school students with mild disabilities. *Intervention in School & Clinic, 30,* 279. doi:10.1177/105345129503000505

Okolo, C. M., & Bouck, E. C. (2007). Research about assistive technology: 2000-2006. What have we learned? *Journal of Special Education Technology, 22,* 19-33.

Palincsar, A. S. (1986). The role of dialogue in providing scaffolded instruction. *Educational Psychologist, 21,* 73-98. doi:10.1080/00461520.1986.9653025

Palincsar, A. S., & Brown, A. L. (1984). Reciprocal teaching of comprehension-fostering and comprehension-monitoring activities. *Cognition and Instruction, 1,* 117-175. doi:10.1207/s1532690xci0102_1

Patterson, K. B. (2005). Increasing positive outcomes for African-American males in special education with the use of guided notes. *Journal of Negro Education, 74*, 311–320.

Pearson, P. D., & Gallagher, M. C. (1983). The instruction of reading comprehension. *Contemporary Educational Psychology, 8*, 317–344. doi:10.1016/0361-476X(83)90019-X

Phillips, C. L., & Vollmer, T. R. (2012). Generalized instruction following with pictorial prompts. *Journal of Applied Behavior Analysis, 45*, 37–54. doi:10.1901/jaba.2012.45-37

Prater, M. A., Carter, N., Hitchcock, C., & Dowrick, P. (2012). Video self-modeling to improve academic performance: A literature review. *Psychology in the Schools, 49*, 71–81. doi:10.1002/pits.20617

Pullen, P. C., Tuckwiller, E. D., Konold, T., Maynard, K., & Coyne, M. (2010). A response to intervention model for vocabulary instruction: The effects of tiered instruction for students at risk for reading disability. *Learning Disabilities Research & Practice, 25*, 110–123. doi:10.1111/j.1540-5826.2010.00309.x

Putambecker. S., & Hübscher, R (2005). Tools for scaffolding students in a complex learning environment: What have we gained and what have we missed? *Educational Psychologist, 40*, 1–12. doi:10.1207/s15326985ep4001_1

Rao, K., Ok, M. W., & Bryant, B. R. (2014). A review of research on universal design educational models. *Remedial and Special Education, 35*, 153–166. doi:10.1177/0741932513518980

REL Southeast. (2011, January). *Measuring student engagement in upper elementary through high school: A description of 21 instruments* (Issues & Answers, REL 2011–No. 098). Washington, DC: Institute of Education Sciences, National Center for Education Evaluation and Regional Assistance, U.S. Department of Education. Retrieved from http://ies.ed.gov/ncee/edlabs/regions/southeast/pdf/rel_2011098.pdf

Rose, D., Meyer, A., & Hitchcock, C. (2005). *The universally designed classroom: Accessibile curriculum and digital technologies.* Cambridge, MA: Harvard Education Press.

Rosenshine, B. (1976). Recent research on teaching behaviors and student achievement. *Journal of Teacher Education, 27*, 61–64. doi:10.1177/002248717602700115

Rosenshine, B. (1983). Teaching functions in instructional programs. *The Elementary School Journal, 83*, 335–351. doi:10.1086/461321

Rosenshine, B. (2012). Principles of instruction: Research-based strategies that all teachers should know. *American Educator, 39*, 12–19.

Rosenshine, B., & Meister, C. (1992). The use of scaffolds for teaching higher-level cognitive strategies. *Educational Leadership, 49*(7), 26-33.

Rosenshine, B., & Stevens, R. (1986). Teaching functions. In M. C. Wittrock (Ed.), *Handbook of research on teaching* (3rd ed., pp. 376-391). New York, NY: Macmillan.

Rumberger, R.W. (2011). *Dropping out: Why students drop out of high school and what can be done about it.* Cambridge, Massachusetts: Harvard University Press.

Santangelo, T., Harris, K. R., & Graham, S. (2007). Self-regulated strategy development: A validated model to support students who struggle with writing. *Learning Disabilities: A Contemporary Journal, 5*, 1-20.

Santangelo, T., Harris, K. R., & Graham, S. (2008). Using self-regulated strategy development to support students who have "trubol giting thangs into werds." *Remedial and Special Education, 29*, 78-89. doi:10.1177/0741932507311636

Schindler, H. S., & Horner, R. H. (2005). Generalized reduction of challenging behavior of young children with autism: Building transituational interventions. *American Journal on Mental Retardation, 110*, 36-47. doi:10.1352/0895-8017(2005)110<36:GROPBO>2.0.CO;2

Schumm, J. S., Moody, S. W., & Vaughn, S. (2000). Grouping for reading instruction: Does one size fit all? *Journal of Learning Disabilities, 33*, 477-488. doi:10.1177/002221940003300508

Schumm, J. S., & Vaughn, S. (1992). Planning for mainstreamed special education students: Perceptions of general education students. *Exceptionality, 3*, 81-98. doi:10.1080/09362839209524799

Schumm, J. S., Vaughn, S., & Saumell, L. (1992). What teachers do when the textbook is tough: Students speak out. *Journal of Reading Behavior, 24*, 481-503. doi:10.1080/10862969209547792

Scott, T. M., Hirn, R. G., & Alter, P. G. (2014). Teacher instruction as a predictor for student engagement and disruptive behaviors. *Preventing School Failure, 58*, 193-200. doi:10.1080/1045988X.2013.787588

Scruggs, T. E., & Mastropieri, M. A. (1989). Mnemonic instruction of LD students: A field based evaluation. *Learning Disability Quarterly, 12*, 119-125. doi:10.2307/1510727

Scruggs, T. E., & Mastropieri, M. A. (1991). Classroom applications of mnemonic instruction: Acquisition, maintenance, and generalization. *Exceptional Children, 58*, 219-229. doi:10.1177/001440299105800305

Scruggs, T. E., & Mastropieri, M. A. (2000). The effectiveness of mnemonic instruction for students with learning and behavior problems: An update and research synthesis. *Journal of Behavioral Education, 10*, 163–173. doi:10.1023/A:1016640214368

Scruggs, T. E., Mastropieri, M. A., McLoone, B. B., Levin, J. R., & Morrison, C. R. (1987). Mnemonic facilitation of learning disabled students' memory for expository prose. *Journal of Educational Psychology, 79*, 27-34. doi:10.1037/0022-0663.79.1.27

Silber, J. M., & Martens, B. K. (2010). Programming for the generalization of oral reading fluency: Repeated readings of entire text versus multiple exemplars. *Journal of Behavioral Education, 19*, 30–46. doi:10.1007/s10864-010-9099-0

Simmons, D. C., Fuchs, L. S., Fuchs, D., Mathes, P., & Hodge, J. P. (1995). Effects of explicit teaching and peer tutoring on the reading achievement of learning-disabled and low-performing students in regular classrooms. *Elementary School Journal, 95*, 387–408. doi:10.1086/461851

Skinner, E. A. & Belmont, M. J. (1993). Motivation in the classroom: Reciprocal effects of teacher behavior and student engagement across the school year. *Journal of Educational Psychology, 85*, 571-581. doi:10.1037/0022-0663.85.4.571

Skinner, E. A., Kindermann, T. A., & Furrer, C. J. (2008). A motivational perspective on engagement and disaffection: Conceptualization and assessment of children's behavioral and emotional participation in academic activities in the classroom. *Educational and Psychological Measurement, 69*, 493–525. doi:10.1177/0013164408323233

Slavin, R. E. (1987). Ability grouping and student achievement in elementary schools: A best evidence synthesis. *Review of Educational Research, 57*, 293–336.

Slavin, R. E. (1990). Achievement effects of ability grouping in secondary schools: A best evidence synthesis. *Review of Educational Research, 60*, 471–499. doi:10.3102/00346543060003471

Smith, J. M., Saez, L., & Doabler, C. T. (2016). Using explicit and systematic instruction to support working memory. *TEACHING Exceptional Children, 48*, 275-281. doi:10.1177/0040059916650633

Smith, S. J., & Okolo, C. (2010). Response to intervention and evidence-based practices: Where does technology fit? *Learning Disability Quarterly, 33*, 257–272. doi:10.1177/073194871003300404

Spencer, D., & Higbee, T. S. (2012). Using transfer of stimulus control technology to promote generalization and spontaneity of language. *Focus on Autism and Other Developmental Disabilities, 27*, 225-236. doi:10.1177/1088357612460274

Stanovich, K. E. (1994). Constructivism in reading education. *The Journal of Special Education, 28,* 259–274. doi:10.1177/002246699402800303

Stevens, R. J., & Slavin, R. E. (1990). When cooperative learning improves the achievement of students with mild disabilities: A response to Tateyama-Sniezek. *Exceptional Children, 57,* 276–280. doi:10.1177/001440299105700311

Stokes, T. F., & Baer, D. M. (1977). An implicit technology of generalization. *Journal of Applied Behavior Analysis, 10,* 349–367. doi:10.1901/jaba.1977.10-349

Swanson, E., Hairrell, A., Kent, S., Ciullo, S., Wanzak, J. A., & Vaughn, S. (2014). A synthesis and meta-analysis of reading interventions using social studies content for students with learning disabilities. *Journal of Learning Disabilities, 47,* 178–195. doi:10.1177/0022219412451131

Swanson, H. L. (2000). What instruction works for students with learning disabilities? Summarizing the results from a meta-analysis of intervention studies. In R. M. Gersten, E. P. Schiller, & S. Vaughn (Eds.), *Contemporary special education research: Syntheses of the knowledge base on critical instructional issues* (pp. 1–30). Mahwah, NJ: Erlbaum.

Sweeney, W. J., Ehrhardt, A. M., Gardner, R., III, Jones, L., Greenfield, R., & Fribley, S. (1999). Using guided notes with academically at-risk high school students during a remedial summer social studies class. *Psychology in the Schools, 36,* 305–318. doi:10.1002/(SICI)1520-6807(199907)36:4<305::AID-PITS4>3.0.CO;2-2

Taylor, B. M., Pearson, P. D., Clark, K. F., & Walpole, S. (2000). Effective schools and accomplished teachers: Lessons about primary-grade reading instruction in low-income schools. *Elementary School Journal, 101,* 121-164. doi:10.1086/499662

Tennessee Curriculum Center. (2011–2016). *Curriculum maps and pacing guides.* Retrieved from http://www.tncurriculumcenter.org/20-stem-tools/standards/curriculum-mapping-guide

Thurlings, M., Vermeulen, M., Bastiaens, T., & Stijnen, S. (2013). Understanding feedback: A learning theory perspective. *Educational Research Review, 9,* 1–15. doi:10.1016/j.edurev.2012.11.004

U.S. Department of Education. (2008). *Foundations for success: The final report of the National Mathematics Advisory Panel.* Retrieved from https://www2.ed.gov/about/bdscomm/list/mathpanel/report/final-report.pdf

U.S. Department of Education. (2016, July). *Notice of proposed rulemaking.* Retrieved from https://www2.ed.gov/policy/elsec/leg/essa/nprmassessementfedreg1a.pdf

Vasquez, O. V., & Caraballo, J. N. (1993, August). *Meta-analysis of the effectiveness of concept mapping as a learning strategy in science education*. Paper presented at the Third International Seminar on the Misconceptions and Educational Strategies in Science and Mathematics Education, Ithaca, NY.

Vaughn, S., & Bos, C. S. (2012). *Strategies for teaching students with learning and behavior problems* (8th ed.). Upper Saddle River, NJ: Pearson.

Vaughn, S., Danielson, L., Zumetta, R., & Holdheide, L. (2015, August). *Deeper learning for students with disabilities* (Deeper Learning Research Series). Boston, MA: Jobs for the Future.

Vaughn, S., Gersten, R., & Chard, D. J. (2000). The underlying message in LD intervention research: Findings from research syntheses. *Exceptional Children, 67*, 99–114. doi:10.1177/001440290006700107

Vaughn, S., Klingner, J. K., Swanson, E. A., Boardman, A. G., Roberts, G., Mohammed, S. S., & Stillman-Spisak, S. J. (2011). Efficacy of collaborative strategic reading with middle school students. *American Educational Research Journal, 48*, 938–964. doi:10.3102/0002831211410305

Vaughn, S., Linan-Thompson, S., Kouzekanani, K., Bryant, D., Dickson, S., & Blozis, S. (2003). Reading instruction grouping for students with reading difficulties. *Remedial and Special Education, 24*, 301–315. doi:10.1177/07419325030240050501

Vaughn, S., Wanzek, J., Murray, C. S., & Roberts, G. (2012). *Intensive interventions for students struggling in reading and mathematics: A practice guide*. Portsmouth, NH: RMC Research Corporation, Center on Instruction. Retrieved from http://files.eric.ed.gov/fulltext/ED531907.pdf

Vygotsky, L. S. (1978). *Mind in society: The development of higher psychological processes*. Cambridge, MA: Harvard University Press.

Weng, P., Maeda, Y., & Bouck, E. C. (2014). Effectiveness of cognitive skills-based computer-assisted instruction for students with disabilities: A synthesis. *Remedial and Special Education, 35*, 167–180. doi:10.1177/0741932513514858

Wharton-MacDonald, R., Pressley, M., & Hampton, J. M. (1998). Literacy instruction in nine first grade classrooms: Teacher characteristics and student achievement. *Elementary School Journal, 99*, 101–128. doi:10.1086/461918

What Works Clearinghouse. (2009a, February). *Assisting students struggling in reading: Response to intervention (RtI) and multi-tier intervention in the primary grades* (NCEE 2009-4045). Washington, DC: National Center for Education Evaluation and Regional Assistance, Institute of Education Sciences, U.S. Department of Education. Retrieved from https://ies.ed.gov/ncee/wwc/Docs/PracticeGuide/rti_reading_pg_021809.pdf

What Works Clearinghouse. (2009b, April). *Assisting students struggling with mathematics: Response to Intervention (RtI) for elementary and middle schools* (NCEE 2009-4060). Washington, DC: National Center for Education Evaluation and Regional Assistance, Institute of Education Sciences, U.S. Department of Education. Retrieved from http://ies.ed.gov/ncee/wwc/Docs/PracticeGuide/rti_math_pg_042109.pdf

What Works Clearinghouse. (2010b, September). *Reciprocal teaching* (WWC Intervention Report). Washington, DC: Institute of Education Sciences, U.S. Department of Education. Retrieved from http://ies.ed.gov/ncee/wwc/Docs/InterventionReports/wwc_rec_teach_091410.pdf

What Works Clearinghouse. (2012, June). *Educator's practice guide: Teaching elementary school students to be effective writers* (NCEE 2012-4058). Washington, DC: National Center for Education Evaluation and Regional Assistance, Institute of Education Sciences, U.S. Department of Education. Retrieved from http://ies.ed.gov/ncee/wwc/Docs/practiceguide/writing_pg_062612.pdf

What Works Clearinghouse. (2014, April). *Educator's practice guide: Teaching academic content and literacy to English learners in elementary and middle school* (NCEE 2014-4012). Washington, DC: Institute of Education Sciences, U.S. Department of Education.

Wolgemuth, J. R., Cobb, R. B., & Alwell, M. (2008). The effects of mnemonic interventions on academic outcomes for youth with disabilities. *Learning Disabilities Research & Practice, 23,* 1–10. doi:10.1111/j.1540-5826.2007.00258.x

Wood, D., Bruner, J., & Ross, G. (1976). The role of tutoring in problem solving. *Journal of Child Psychology and Child Psychiatry, 17,* 89–100. doi:10.1111/j.1469-7610.1976.tb00381.x

Appendix
Glossary of Terms
and Related Resources

Term	Definition	Reference/Resource
Academic learning time	"Allocated time in a subject-matter area (physical education, science, or mathematics, for example) in which a student is engaged successfully in the activities or with the materials to which he or she is exposed, and in which those activities and materials are related to educational outcomes that are valued."	EduTechWiki (2007)
Adapting instruction	Changes to classroom instruction in order to allow students equal access to the curriculum and to give students the opportunity to both process and demonstrate what has been taught; instructional adaptations can include both accommodations and modifications.	The IRIS Center (2005, Page 8)

Term	Definition	Reference/Resource
Assistive technology	"Any item, piece of equipment, or product system, whether acquired commercially off the shelf, modified, or customized, that is used to increase, maintain, or improve the functional capabilities of a child with a disability."	IDEA, 20 U.S.C. § 1401(1)
	Schools are required to consider assistive technology for students with disabilities when developing students' IEPs.	34 C.F.R. § 300.346(2) (v)
		Parette, Peterson-Karlan, Wojcik, & Bardi (2007)
Augmentative and alternative communication systems (AAC)	Alternative methods of communication, which may include communication boards, communication books, sign language, and computerized voices, used by individuals unable to communicate readily through speech.	Alper & Raharinirina (2006)
Benchmark	"A typical or expected performance level in a given skill (e.g., reading) that serves as a general indicator of a student's overall progress."	The IRIS Center (2016a)
Choral responding	Instructional activity in which all of the students in a group provide a response in unison.	Intervention Central (n.d.)

Term	Definition	Reference/Resource
Collaboration	"A style for direct interaction between at least two coequal parties voluntarily engaged in shared decision making as they work toward a common goal."	Friend & Cook (2017, p. 5)
	In educational settings this typically includes "planning, implementing, or evaluating a specific aspect of an educational program for a student or group of students."	The IRIS Center (2007, Page 3)
		Friend & Cook (2017); Friend, Cook, Hurley-Chamberlain, & Shamberger (2010); The IRIS Center (2004c)
Collaborative strategic reading (CSR)	A multi-component approach to reading improvement in which students apply comprehension strategies while reading expository text in small cooperative learning groups.	The IRIS Center (2008a, Page 3)

Term	Definition	Reference/Resource
Comprehensive learner profile	Provides information about a students' academic, social and emotional, functional and motivation strengths and needs as a means of establishing how a student learns best (i.e., how the student gathers, processes, and applies information). Includes information about a students' interests, culture, and language. Teachers use the comprehensive learner profile to craft a robust IEP. In developing the profile, teachers collect and analyze a variety of both summative and formative data gathered from a variety of sources including teachers, administrators, parents, related service providers, and community stakeholders.	Inclusive Education Planning Tool (2011); National Joint Committee on Learning Disabilities (2010)
Content enhancements	Strategies to augment the organization and delivery of curriculum content so that students can better access, interact with, understand, and retain information.	Deshler et al. (2001)
Content scaffolding	Instructional strategy in which educators teach material that is not too difficult or unfamiliar to students learning a new skill.	The IRIS Center (2004b, Page 3)
Cooperative learning	Students of mixed ability levels are arranged into small groups and rewarded based on their collective performance. Cooperative learning includes positive interdependence, individual accountability, equality participation, and simultaneous interactions.	U.S. Department of Education Office of Research (1992)
Corrective feedback	Constructive comments provided as soon as possible following the implementation of an activity in order to help an individual improve his or her performance.	Archer & Hughes (2011)

Term	Definition	Reference/Resource
Co-teaching	"The partnering of a general education teacher and a special education teacher or another specialist for the purpose of jointly delivering instruction to a diverse group of students, including those with disabilities, or other special needs, in a general education setting and in a way that flexibly and deliberately meets their learning needs."	Friend, Hurley-Chamberlain, & Shamberger (2010, p. 11)
Culturally relevant practices	Instruction that incorporates the diverse cultures of the students in order to provide content relative to students' experiences.	Aronson & Laughter (2016)
Curriculum-based assessment (CBA)	"A method of evaluating student performance by directly and frequently collecting data on their academic progress."	The IRIS Center (2016a)
Curriculum-based measurement (CBM)	"A type of progress monitoring conducted on a regular basis to assess student performance throughout an entire year's curriculum; teachers can use CBM to evaluate not only student progress but also the effectiveness of their instructional methods."	The IRIS Center (2016a)
Data-based individualization	Gradually individualizing and intensifying interventions through the systematic use of assessment data, validated interventions, and research-based adaptation strategies.	National Center on Intensive Intervention (2013)

Term	Definition	Reference/Resource
Differentiated instruction	"An approach whereby teachers adjust their curriculum and instruction to maximize the learning of all students (e.g., typical learners, English language learners, struggling students, students with learning disabilities, gifted and talented students); not a single strategy but rather a framework that teachers can use to implement a variety of evidence-based strategies."	The IRIS Center (2010a, Page 1)
Disproportionality	The over- or underrepresentation "of racially, culturally, ethnically, or linguistically diverse groups of students in special education, restrictive learning environments, or school disciplinary actions (e.g., suspensions and expulsions), compared to other groups."	Center on Response to Intervention (2014)
	Per IDEA, states must have "policies and procedures designed to prevent the inappropriate overidentification or disproportionate representation by race and ethnicity of children as children with disabilities."	U.S. Department of Education (2007)
Evidence-based practice	Educational practice or strategy that has empirical evidence to support its efficacy.	See Council for Exceptional Children (2014)
Explicit instruction	Instructional approach in which teachers clearly identify the expectations for learning, highlight important details of the concept or skill, offer precise instruction, and connect new learning to earlier lessons and materials.	Archer & Hughes (2011)
Fidelity of implementation	"The degree to which an intervention is implemented accurately, following the guidelines or restrictions of its developers."	The IRIS Center (2016a)

Term	Definition	Reference/Resource
Flexible grouping	A fluid or dynamic method of grouping students. Rather than being set, group membership changes to meet the different needs of the students.	Cox (n.d.)
Formative assessment	A form of formal or informal evaluation "used to plan instruction in a recursive way," providing regular assessment of student progress. Formative assessment enables teachers to "diagnose skill, ability, and knowledge gaps; measure progress; and evaluate instruction. Examples … include curriculum-based measurement, curriculum-based assessment, pretests and posttests, portfolios, benchmark assessments, quizzes, teacher observations, and teacher/student conferencing."	Center on Response to Intervention (2014)
Functional behavior assessment (FBA)	A systematic approach to address a student's specific behavior to identify the behavior's function using informal and formal methods of observation. Following the FBA, the IEP team develops an individual behavior support plan.	Behavioradvisor.com (n.d.)
Generalization	Performing a behavior in environments that differ from where the behavior was originally learned.	Lee & Axelrod (2005).
Grade equivalence	Grade-level equivalent scores are determined by giving a test that is developed for a particular grade to students in other grades.	Eissenberg & Rudner (1988)
Graphic organizer	A visual aid designed to help students organize and comprehend substantial amounts of text and content information.	The IRIS Center (2012, Page 11)

Term	Definition	Reference/Resource
Guided notes	"A strategic note-taking method in which teachers provide their students an outline containing the main ideas and related concepts in order to help guide the students through a lecture."	The IRIS Center (2016a)
Guided practice	A method of practice that involves working with students on activities that focus on a previously modeled or taught skill.	Study.com (2003–2017)
Heterogeneous grouping	To place students of varying abilities (i.e., lower achieving, typically achieving, higher achieving) together in a small instructional group.	Lewis (2016a)
Homogeneous grouping	To place students of similar abilities together into groups; can be used by teachers to provide more intensive instruction to students who are working at a similar level and who can benefit from instruction that is designed for their specific learning needs.	Lewis (2016b)
Individual behavior support plan	A plan developed following a functional behavior assessment to specify how the pro-social behavior will be taught and any modifications to the classroom and other environments needed to reinforce the appropriate behavior.	See OSEP Technical Assistance Center's templates at https://www.pbis.org/resource/804/behavior-support-plan-template
Individual family services plan (IFSP)	A means of providing early intervention services for children with developmental delays or disabilities, from birth through age 3. The IFSP is based on an in-depth assessment of the child's needs and includes information on the child's level of development in all areas, outcomes for the child and family, and services the child and family will receive.	PACER Center (2011)

Term	Definition	Reference/Resource
Individualized education program (IEP)	A written statement for the child with a disability that is developed, reviewed, and revised in a meeting in accordance with federal law and regulations. The IEP must include a statement of the child's present levels of academic achievement and functional performance, a statement of measurable annual academic and functional goals to meet the child's needs and enable the child to make progress in the general education curriculum.	IDEA regulations, 34 C.F.R. § 300.320–300.324 See U.S. Department of Education (2006)
Instructional scaffolding	"A process through which a teacher adds supports for students to enhance learning and aid in the mastery of tasks. The teacher does this by systematically building on students' experiences and knowledge as they are learning new skills."	The IRIS Center (2005, Page 1)
Instructional technology	"Any device or instrument that exists in a classroom and that teachers use for the purpose of day-to-day instruction; such devices, when assigned to an individual student through an IEP, are known as assistive technology."	The IRIS Center (2016a)
Intensive intervention	Additional instruction designed to support and reinforce classroom skills characterized by increased intensity and individualization based on data.	The IRIS Center (2015, Page 1)
Key word method	A mnemonic strategy in which students use a keyword and a related sentence or image to help them to remember new information.	Mempowered! (n.d.)
Learning strategies	"Instructional methods employed to help students to read, comprehend, and study better by helping them to strategically organize and collect information."	The IRIS Center (2016a)

Term	Definition	Reference/Resource
Maintenance	In behavior assessment, term used to describe the extent to which a student's behavior is self-sustaining over time.	Potterfield (2009–2013)
Meta-analysis	Method of reviewing research on a given practice or program in which a systematic and reproducible literature search is conducted, specific criteria are used for including research studies in the analysis, and the combined statistical results of these studies yield an effect size for the practice or program across the studies reviewed.	Israel & Richter (2017)
Metacognition	The processes used to plan, monitor, and assess one's understanding and performance.	Chick (2017)
Mnemonics	"A learning strategy in which a verbal device is employed to help promote the memorization of names or other information."	The IRIS Center (2016a)
Multitiered system of support (MTSS)	A "prevention framework that organizes building-level resources to address each individual student's academic and/or behavioral needs within intervention tiers that vary in intensity." The intention is to enable "the early identification of learning and behavioral challenges and timely intervention for students who are at risk for poor learning outcomes. It also may be called a *multi-level prevention system*. The increasingly intense tiers … represent a continuum of supports."	Center on Response to Intervention (2014)
Norm-referenced assessment	"A standardized assessment tool that compares a student's test scores to the average score of a representative group."	The IRIS Center (2016a)

Term	Definition	Reference/Resource
Paraprofessional	Sometimes also referred to as a paraeducator, teacher's aide, or instructional assistant, a paraprofessional may assist in providing special education and related services to students with disabilities. They are appropriately trained and supervised in accordance with state law, regulation, or written policy.	IDEA, 20 U.S.C. 1412(a)(14)(b); see Giangreco, Suter, & Doyle (2010)
Peer tutoring	A cooperative learning strategy that pairs a student with disabilities with a typically developing student; either student may adopt the role of teacher or learner.	The IRIS Center (2010b, Page 7)
Pegword strategy	A *mnemonic* strategy in which students use common rhyming words for numbers (e.g., one = bun; two = shoe) and link this word to the information being learned.	AdLit.org (2017)
Progress monitoring	Used to assess a student's performance and improvement in response to intervention. Allows teachers to evaluate the effectiveness of interventions adjust instruction to meet students' needs. Progress monitoring can be implemented with individual students or groups of students (e.g., whole class).	Center on Response to Intervention (2014); The IRIS Center (2004a, Page 1); Stockall, Dennis, & Rueter (2014)
Reciprocal teaching	"Instructional activity in which students become the teacher in small group sessions. Teachers model, then help students learn to guide group discussions using four strategies: summarizing, question generating, clarifying, and predicting."	Reading Rockets (2017)
Scientifically validated interventions	"Instructional procedures or methods proven by careful and systematic research."	The IRIS Center (2016a)

Term	Definition	Reference/Resource
Self-regulated strategy development	A scientifically validated framework for explicitly teaching academic strategies that incorporates steps critical to a student's ability to effectively use those strategies.	The IRIS Center (2008b)
Self-regulation	"A person's ability to regulate his or her own behavior. "	The IRIS Center (2016a)
Special education process	The activities that occur from the time a child is referred for evaluation through being identified with a disability and provided with special education services via an IEP. These activities include request for an evaluation, a multidisciplinary evaluation, eligibility determination, and the development of the IEP. Families of students who are being evaluated must be informed of all activities and have opportunities to participate in meetings and decisions about their child.	Center for Parent Information and Resources (2014); PACER Center (2006)
Strategies instruction	Instruction designed to teach students the elements or steps for implementing successful strategies.	Gaskins, 2009
Summative assessment	"An evaluation administered to measure student learning outcomes, typically at the end of a unit or chapter. Often used to evaluate whether a student has mastered the content or skill."	The IRIS Center (2016a)
Targeted instruction	Instruction that "takes into account what students understand and teaches them according to their ability levels, rather than strictly adhering to what they are expected to know based on their grade level."	Center for Education Innovations (n.d.)

Term	Definition	Reference/Resource
Testing accommodations	A change in the way that a test is administered or responded to by the person being tested. Accommodations are intended to offset or "correct" for distortions in scores caused by a disability. These changes do not modify the intent of the test. Allowable accommodations may include such things as extended time, use of read-aloud software, text-to-speech and speech-to-text software, and calculators.	Cawthon et al. (2009); Elliott, Kratochwill, & Schulte (1998); Fuchs & Fuchs (1999); Fuchs, Fuchs, Eaton, Hamlett, & Karns (2000); Kettler et al. (2011)
Transition services	Instruction, related services, and community experiences designed to support the student with a disability in developing academic and functional skills suited to the student's postschool goals. Per federal regulations, this is a results-oriented process that considers including postsecondary education, vocational education, integrated employment (including supported employment), continuing and adult education, adult services, independent living, or community participation, as appropriate for the individual student's needs and taking into consideration the child's strengths, preferences, and interests.	IDEA regulations, 34 C.F.R. § 300.43(a)
Universal design for learning (UDL)	A research-based framework for teachers to incorporate flexible materials, techniques, and strategies for delivering instruction and for students to demonstrate their knowledge in a variety of ways.	The IRIS Center (2016b)

References

Adlit.org. (2017). *Classroom strategies: Mnemonics*. Retrieved from http://www. adlit.org/strategies/22732/

Alper, S., & Raharinirina, S. (2006). Assistive technology for individuals with disabilities: A review and synthesis of the literature. *Journal of Special Education Technology, 21*, 47 -64.

Archer, A. L., & Hughes, C. A. (2011). *Explicit instruction: Effective and efficient teaching*. New York, NY: Guilford.

Aronson, B., & Laughter, J. (2016). The theory and practice of culturally relevant education: A synthesis of research across content areas. *Review of Educational Research, 86*, 163 -205. doi:10.3102/0034654315582066

Behavioradvisor.com. (n.d.) *Functional behavior assessment (FBA)*. Retrieved from http://www.behavioradvisor.com/FBA.html

Cawthon, S. W., Eching, H., Patel, P. G., Potvin, D. C., & Trundt, K. M. (2009) Multiple constructs and effects of accommodations on accommodated test scores for students with disabilities. *Practical Assessment, Research & Evaluation, 14*(18), 1–9. Retrieved from http://pareonline.net/getvn.asp?v=14&n=18

Center for Education Innovations. (n.d.) *Targeted instruction*. Retrieved from http:// www.earlylearningtoolkit.org/content/targeted-instruction

Center for Parent Information and Resources. (2014, May). *Evaluating children for disability*. Newark, NJ: Author. Retrieved from http://www.parentcenterhub. org/repository/evaluation/

Center on Response to Intervention. (2014, March). *Response to intervention glossary of terms*. Washington, DC: American Institutes for Research and National Center on Intensive Intervention. Retrieved from http://www. rti4success.org/sites/default/files/CenterOnRTIGlossary.pdf

Chick, N. (2017). *CFT teaching guide: Metacognition*. Nashville, TN: Vanderbilt University Center for Teaching. Retrieved from https://cft.vanderbilt.edu/ guides-sub-pages/metacognition/

Council for Exceptional Children. (2014). *Standards for evidence-based practices in special education*. Arlington, VA: Author. Retrieved from https://www.cec. sped.org/~/media/Files/Standards/Evidence%20based%20Practices%20 and%20Practice/EBP%20FINAL.pdf

Cox, J. (n.d.) *Flexible grouping as a differentiated instruction strategy*. Retrieved from http://www.teachhub.com/flexible-grouping-differentiated-instruction-strategy

Deshler, D. D., Schumaker, J. B., Bulgren, J. A., Lenz, B. K., Jantzen, J., Adams, G., … Marquis, J. (2001). Making things easier: Connecting knowledge to things students already know. *TEACHING Exceptional Children, 33*(4), 82–85. doi:10.1177/004005990103300412

EduTechWiki. (2007, February). *Instructional time.* Retrieved from http://edutechwiki.unige.ch/en/Instructional_time

Eissenberg, T. E., & Rudner, L. M. (1988, November). Explaining test results to parents. *Practical Assessment, Research & Evaluation, 1*(1). Retrieved from http://PAREonline.net/getvn.asp?v=1&n=1

Elliott, S. N., Kratochwill, T. R., & Schulte, A. G. (1998). The assessment accommodations checklist: Who, what, where, when, why, and how? *TEACHING Exceptional Children, 31*(2), 10–14. doi: 10.1177/004005999803100202

Friend, M., & Cook, L. (2017). *Interactions: Collaboration skills for school professionals* (8th ed.). Upper Saddle River, NJ: Pearson.

Friend, M., Cook, L., Hurley-Chamberlain, D., & Shamberger, C. (2010). Co-teaching: An illustration of the complexity of collaboration in special education. *Journal of Educational and Psychological Consultation, 20*, 9–27. doi:10.1080/10474410903535380

Fuchs, L. S., & Fuchs, D. (1999, November). Fair and unfair testing accommodations. *School Administrator, 56*(10), 24–29.

Fuchs, L. S., Fuchs, D., Eaton, S. B., Hamlett, C., & Karns, K. (2000). Supplementing teacher judgments of test accommodations with objective data sources. *School Psychology Review, 29*, 65–85.

Gaskins, I. (2009, December). *Major approaches to strategies instruction.* Retrieved from http://www.education.com/reference/article/strategies-instruction/

Giangreco, M. F., Suter, J. C., & Doyle, M. B. (2010). Paraprofessionals in inclusive schools: A review of recent research. *Journal of Educational and Psychological Consultation, 20*, 41–57. doi:10.1080/10474410903535356

IDEA regulations, 34 C.F.R. § 300 (2012).

Inclusive Education Planning Tool (IEPT). (2011). *What is a learner profile?* (Action on Inclusion). Alberta, Canada: Parkland School Division. Retrieved from https://sites.google.com/a/fmcsd.ab.ca/inclusive-education-planning-tool-iept/learner-profiles

Individuals With Disabilities Education Act, 20 U.S.C. §§ 1400 *et seq.* (2006 & Supp. V. 2011)

Intervention Central. (n.d.). *Group-response techniques*. Retrieved from http://www.interventioncentral.org/academic-interventions/general-academic/group-response-techniques

The IRIS Center. (2004a). *Classroom assessment (Part 1): An introduction to monitoring academic achievement in the classroom* [Training module]. Nashville, TN: Peabody College, Vanderbilt University. Retrieved from http://iris.peabody.vanderbilt.edu/module/gpm/#content

The IRIS Center. (2004b). *Content standards: Connecting standards-based curriculum to instructional planning* [Training module]. Nashville, TN: Peabody College, Vanderbilt University. Retrieved from http://iris.peabody.vanderbilt.edu/module/sca/

The IRIS Center. (2004c). *Effective school practices: Promoting collaboration and monitoring students' academic achievement* [Training module]. Nashville, TN: Peabody College, Vanderbilt University. Retrieved from http://iris.peabody.vanderbilt.edu/module/esp/

The IRIS Center. (2005). *Providing instructional supports: Facilitating mastery of new skills* [Training module]. Nashville, TN: Peabody College, Vanderbilt University. Retrieved from http://iris.peabody.vanderbilt.edu/module/cnm/

The IRIS Center. (2007). *Serving students with visual impairments: The importance of collaboration* [Training module]. Nashville, TN: Peabody College, Vanderbilt University. Retrieved from http://iris.peabody.vanderbilt.edu/module/v03-focusplay/

The IRIS Center. (2008a). *CSR: A reading comprehension strategy* [Training module]. Nashville, TN: Peabody College, Vanderbilt University. Retrieved from http://iris.peabody.vanderbilt.edu/module/csr/

The IRIS Center. (2008b). *SRSD: Using learning strategies to enhance student learning* [Training module]. Nashville, TN: Peabody College, Vanderbilt University. Retrieved from http://iris.peabody.vanderbilt.edu/module/srs/

The IRIS Center. (2010a). *Differentiated instruction: Maximizing the learning of all students* [Training module]. Nashville, TN: Peabody College, Vanderbilt University. Retrieved from http://iris.peabody.vanderbilt.edu/module/di/

The IRIS Center. (2010b). *High-quality mathematics instruction: What teachers should know* [Training module]. Nashville, TN: Peabody College, Vanderbilt University. Retrieved from https://iris.peabody.vanderbilt.edu/module/math/

The IRIS Center. (2012). *Secondary reading instruction: Teaching vocabulary and comprehension in the content areas* [Training module]. Nashville, TN: Peabody College, Vanderbilt University. Retrieved from http://iris.peabody.vanderbilt.edu/module/sec-rdng/

The IRIS Center. (2015). *Intensive Intervention (Part 1): Using Data-Based Individualization To Intensify Instruction* [Training module]. Nashville, TN: Peabody College, Vanderbilt University. Retrieved from http://iris.peabody. vanderbilt.edu/module/dbi1/

The IRIS Center. (2016a). *Glossary.* Nashville, TN: Peabody College, Vanderbilt University. Retrieved from http://iris.peabody.vanderbilt.edu/glossary/

The IRIS Center. (2016b). *Universal design for learning: Creating a learning environment that challenges and engages all students* [Training module]. Nashville, TN: Peabody College, Vanderbilt University. Retrieved from http:// iris.peabody.vanderbilt.edu/module/udl/

Israel, H., & Richter, R. R. (2017). A guide to understanding meta-analysis. *Journal of Orthopaedic & Sports Physical Therapy, 41,* 496-504.

Kagan, S., & Kagan, M. (2009). *Kagan cooperative learning.* San Clemente, CA: Kagan Publishing.

Kettler, R. J., Rodriguez, M. C., Bolt, D. M., Elliott, S. N., Beddow, P. A., & Kurz, A. (2011). Modified multiple-choice items for alternate assessments: Reliability, difficulty, and differential boost. *Applied Measurement In Education, 24,* 210–234. doi:10.1080/08957347.2011.580620

Lee, D. L., & Axelrod, S. A. (2005). *Behavior modification: Basic principles* (3rd ed.). Austin, TX: PRO-ED.

Lewis, B. (2016a, September). *Heterogeneous groups.* Retrieved from http:// k6educators.about.com/od/educationglossary/g/gheterogeneous.htm

Lewis, B. (2016b, September). *Homogeneous groups.* Retrieved from http:// k6educators.about.com/od/educationglossary/g/ghomogeneous.htm

Mempowered! (n.d.). *Keyword method.* Retrieved from http://www.mempowered. com/strategies/keyword-method

National Center on Intensive Intervention. (2013, March). *Data-based individualization: A framework for intensive intervention.* Washington, DC: Office of Special Education, U.S. Department of Education. Retrieved from http://www.intensiveintervention.org/sites/default/files/DBI_Framework.pdf

National Joint Committee on Learning Disabilities. (2010). *Comprehensive assessment and evaluation of students with learning disabilities.* Retrieved from http://www.ldonline.org/article/54711/

PACER Center. (2006). *Understanding the special education process: An overview for parents* (Action Information Sheet). Minneapolis, MN: Author. Retrieved from http://www.pacer.org/publications/pdfs/ALL17.pdf

PACER Center. (2011). *What is the difference between an IFSP and an IEP?* (Action Information Sheet). Minneapolis, MN: Author. Retrieved from http://www.pacer.org/parent/php/PHP-c59.pdf

Parette, H. P., Peterson-Karlan, G. R., Wojcik, B. W., & Bardi, N. (2007). Monitor that progress! Interpreting data trends for assistive technology decision making. *TEACHING Exceptional Children, 40*(1), 22-29. doi:10.1177/004005990704000103

Potterfield, J. (2009-2013). *ABA toolbox: Maintenance.* Retrieved from https://sites.google.com/site/thebcbas/aba-toolbox/maintenance

Reading Rockets. (2017). *Reciprocal teaching.* Retrieved from http://www.readingrockets.org/strategies/reciprocal_teaching

Stockall, N., Dennis, L. R., & Reuter, J. A. (2014). Developing a progress monitoring portfolio for children in early childhood special education programs. *TEACHING Exceptional Children, 46*(3), 32-40. doi:10.1177/004005991404600304

Study.com. (2003-2017). Providing guided practice & models in instruction. *Effective Instructional Strategies for Teachers.* Retrieved from http://study.com/academy/lesson/providing-guided-practice-models-in-instruction.html

U.S. Department of Education. (2006, October 4). *IDEA regulations: Individualized education program (IEP).* Retrieved from http://idea.ed.gov/explore/view/p/%2Croot%2Cdynamic%2CTopicalBrief%2C10%2C

U.S. Department of Education. (2007, February 2). *IDEA regulations: Disproportionality and overidentification.* Retrieved from http://idea.ed.gov/explore/view/p/,root,dynamic,TopicalBrief,7,

U.S. Department of Education Office of Research. (1992, June). Cooperative learning. *Education Consumer Guide.* Retrieved from https://www2.ed.gov/pubs/OR/ConsumerGuides/cooplear.html